SELECTION
EXAMINATION
ENGLISH
TESTS

BY

HAYDN RICHARDS

GINN AND COMPANY LTD

By the same Author

JUNIOR ENGLISH REVISED
JUNIOR ENGLISH GUIDE
HAYDN RICHARDS ENGLISH WORKBOOKS
HAYDN RICHARDS JUNIOR ENGLISH
VERBAL REASONING TESTS EXPLAINED
MORE VERBAL REASONING TESTS

First Published 1956
Thirty-third impression 1983   158308
ISBN 0 602 20860 2

Published by Ginn and Company Ltd
Prebendal House, Parson's Fee, Aylesbury, Bucks HP20 2QZ

Printed in Great Britain at the University Press, Oxford
by Eric Buckley, Printer to the University

PREFACE

As its title implies this book has been specially designed to test the ability in English of children who intend sitting for the Selection Examination.

Planned after a careful study of examination papers set by various Education Authorities, the book contains 30 complete tests, each of which is divided into seven sections lettered A to G.

In each test Section A is a Comprehension Test, Section G is a Composition Exercise, whilst the remaining sections are devoted to Grammar, Spelling, Vocabulary, Sentence Construction, Punctuation, Figures of Speech, etc., topics which appear in most Selection Examination English papers.

The time allowed for each complete test should be $1\frac{1}{4}$ hours, and the following allocation of marks is suggested in assessing the pupil's total marks.

		Total
Section A	Comprehension	
	3 marks for each correct answer	30

Sections B to F—10 marks for each section

If 5 questions—2 marks each	
If 10 questions—1 mark each	50
If 20 questions—$\frac{1}{2}$ mark each	

Section G	Composition	20
		100

CONTENTS

Test	Title of Comprehension Exercise	Page
1.	Pirates	7
2.	The Runaway Camel	11
3.	Maggie and the Gypsies	15
4.	Hurricane	19
5.	Father William	23
6.	The Horse Fair	27
7.	The Artful Dodger	31
8.	A Thrilling Escape	35
9.	The Shepherd	39
10.	Bird Fights	43
11.	Rip Van Winkle	47
12.	The Hovel	51
13.	Trading With Eskimos	55
14.	Whitewashing	58
15.	Tom and the Keeper	62
16.	The Giant Roc	66
17.	The Little Duke's Escape	70
18.	A Brazilian Forest	74
19.	Tickler	78
20.	Taken By Surprise	82
21.	The New Home	86
22.	Big-end Versus Little-end	90
23.	The Court of Justice	94
24.	The Hunter	98
25.	Humphrey to the Rescue	102
26.	Romulus and Remus	106
27.	The Rival Schools	111
28.	The Wild Man of Treasure Island	115
29.	The Crowning of Arthur	120
30.	The New Scrooge	125

A

Comprehension

(Read this passage through very carefully, then answer
the questions which follow.)

PIRATES

With joyful anticipation of rescue we hastened to the highest
point of rock and awaited the arrival of the vessel, for we now
perceived that she was making straight for the island.

In less than an hour she was close to the reef, where she stopped
to survey the coast. Seeing this, and fearing that they might not
see us, we waved pieces of cloth in the air, and soon had the satisfaction of seeing them beginning to lower a boat and bustle about
the decks as if they meant to land. Suddenly a flag was run up
at the peak, a little cloud of white smoke rose from the schooner's
side, and before we could guess their intentions a cannon-shot
came crashing through the bushes, carried away several coconut
trees in its passage, and burst in atoms against the cliff a few yards
below the spot on which we stood.

With feelings of terror we observed that the flag at the schooner's
peak was black, with a death's-head and cross-bones on it. As
we gazed at each other in blank astonishment the word "pirate"
escaped our lips simultaneously.

The Coral Island by R. M. Ballantyne

(The "we" in this story refers to three boys: Jack Martin,
Peterkin Gay and Ralph Rover.)

1. Where did the boys hurry to?
2. Why did they go there?
3. How long did it take the ship to get close to the reef?
4. Why did the boys wave pieces of cloth in the air?

7

5. Why did the boys think that the crew of the ship meant to land?
6. What kind of flag was suddenly hoisted at the ship's peak?
7. What did the boys see rising from the ship's side?
8. Where did the cannon-shot burst?
9. What damage did it do in its passage?
10. Why did the ship stop when it approached the reef?

B Write the words which are missing from these sentences. They all end with —**ght.**

Example: One parcel was heavy; the other was ——.

Answer: light.

1. Frank stayed out in the rain and —— a very bad cold.
2. The concert lasted three hours, from —— o'clock till eleven.
3. The champion's —— for the contest was 92 kilograms.
4. The British troops —— like Trojans and put the enemy to flight.
5. Will has not —— his football to school today.
6. Although she is nearly eleven years old, Gillian is only 127 centimetres in ——.
7. A —— line is the shortest distance between two points.
8. The door was left open, causing a ——.
9. During the long —— most of the crops withered and died.
10. A window in a roof or ceiling is called a ——.

C Copy the names of the countries given below, then write the name of the native opposite each.

Country	Native	Country	Native
1. Wales	Welshman	3. Belgium	——
2. Denmark	——	4. Norway	——

8

Country	Native		Country	Native
5. Greece	——		8. Sweden	——
6. Italy	——		9. Holland	——
7. France	——		10. Portugal	——

 Can you name these characters from literature?

1. The savage who became Robinson Crusoe's manservant.
2. The boy who hid in an apple barrel aboard the ship "Hispaniola".
3. The King whose touch turned everything into gold.
4. The man who rid a town of its rats by playing a tune on his magic pipe.
5. The miser who considered that Christmas was a "humbug".

 Use these ten words to complete the following phrases.

ray	wisp	flake	breath	drop
crumb	pinch	speck	splinter	grain

1. a —— of bread
2. a —— of sand
3. a —— of salt
4. a —— of dust
5. a —— of straw
6. a —— of wood
7. a —— of snow
8. a —— of sunshine
9. a —— of water
10. a —— of air

F Join each set of three sentences to form one sentence, using the connecting words in brackets.

Example: Mother got up from her chair. She handed me my stockings. She had just darned them. (and, which)

Answer: Mother got up from her chair and handed me my stockings which she had just darned.

1. I returned to the pavilion. There I found Dick. He had just been bowled for a duck. (where, who)

9

2. Mrs Archer made the pastry. Jane peeled the apples. Susan fetched the plates. (while, and)

3. The police gave chase. They failed to overtake the bandit. He was travelling at 90 kilometres an hour. (but, who)

4. Bill stopped. He pointed to a dangerous corner. A cyclist had been killed there the previous day. (and, where)

5. Jane was crying. She had lost the silver bangle. Her mother had given it to her for a birthday present. (because, which)

G Write a composition of about 15 lines on any one of the following subjects.

    1. A Visit To A Circus

    2. A Day At The Seaside

    3. Washing Day

TEST 2

 A

Comprehension

THE RUNAWAY CAMEL

Suddenly the camel shot round a hill, bringing Sailor Bill in full view of a Bedouin encampment, within which he could see the forms of men, women and children. Around were animals of different sorts; horses, camels, sheep, goats and dogs, grouped according to their kind, with the exception of the dogs, which appeared to be straying everywhere.

There were voices, shouting and singing. There was music, made upon some rude instrument, and there were men and women dancing.

Bill had made up his mind to dismount at any cost; but there was no time. Before he could do so he saw that he was discovered, a cry coming from the tents warning him of this fact. It was too late to attempt a retreat, so he decided to stick to the saddle. Not much longer, for the camel, with a snorting scream, rushed into the encampment, right into the very circle of the dancers, and there stopped with such abrupt suddenness that its rider, after performing a somersault through the air, came down on all-fours in front of its projecting snout.

The Boy Slaves by Capt. Mayne Reid

1. What did Bill see after rounding the hill?

2. What did he hear?

3. Which animals were not grouped together?

4. Who were dancing?

5. What had Bill decided to do?

6. Why was he not able to do it?

7. How did Bill know that he had been seen?

8. What did the camel do on reaching the encampment?

9. What effect did this have on Bill?

10. What noise did the camel make as it rushed into the encampment?

B Indicate by the letters (a), (b) or (c) the correct meaning of each of the following idioms.

1. To blow one's own trumpet

    (a) to disturb the peace
    (b) to be boastful
    (c) to demonstrate one's musical ability

2. To show the white feather

    (a) to be in the fashion
    (b) to be an expert archer
    (c) to be a coward

3. To let the cat out of the bag

    (a) to disclose a secret
    (b) to show kindness to dumb creatures
    (c) to interfere in the affairs of other people

4. To bury the hatchet

    (a) to look after one's tools
    (b) to make peace
    (c) to conceal stolen goods

5. To hit below the belt

    (a) to lose one's temper and become reckless
    (b) to act unfairly
    (c) to attempt to cripple an opponent

Fit these verbs into the phrases below:

excavate   denounce   forge   reveal   inherit
abandon   intercept   reserve   accomplish   undergo

1. to —— a secret
2. to —— a sinking ship
3. to —— an operation
4. to —— a task
5. to —— a seat
6. to —— a fortune
7. to —— a trench
8. to —— a signature
9. to —— a pass (football)
10. to —— an impostor

 Complete each of these sentences by inserting one of the words given. One word is used twice.

rise   rose   raise   raised

1. The boys —— their caps as their headmaster passed.
2. The boss promised to —— Tom's wages.
3. Tom has been promised a —— in his wages.
4. The House of Commons —— at 22.50 hours.
5. The comedian's jokes —— many a laugh last night.

E   In each line below find the two words which have opposite meanings.

1. protest, prohibit, praise, permit, rebuke
2. accused, guilty, haughty, innocent, suspected
3. dauntless, reckless, vicious, expert, cautious
4. chase, assist, hinder, pursue, hurry
5. expensive, flawless, genuine, gorgeous, imperfect

13

Copy this figure, then complete the words ending with —**ery**, placing one letter in each blank space.

						e	r	y		
						e	r	y	=	a coalmine and its buildings
						e	r	y	=	a public burial ground
						e	r	y	=	dishes made of earthenware
						e	r	y	=	a room where dishes etc. are washed
						e	r	y	=	exaggerated or untrue praise

 Write a composition of about 15 lines on any one of these subjects.

1. Road Safety
2. My Favourite Television Programme
3. Helping At Home

14

TEST 3

Comprehension

MAGGIE AND THE GYPSIES

It now appeared that the man also was to be seated on the donkey, holding Maggie before him, and she was as unable to object to this plan as the donkey himself, though no nightmare had ever seemed to her more horrible. When the woman had patted her on the back, and said "Good-bye", the donkey, at a strong hint from the man's stick, set off at a rapid walk along the lane to the point Maggie had come from an hour ago, while the tall girl and the rough urchin, also furnished with sticks, obligingly escorted them for the first hundred yards, with much screaming and thwacking.

The Mill On The Floss by George Eliot

1. Who was to accompany Maggie on her ride?
2. Who was to sit nearer the donkey's neck?
3. Did Maggie look forward to the ride with enjoyment?
4. Who wished Maggie "Good-bye"?
5. What made the donkey set off at a rapid walk?
6. Where was the donkey making for?
7. Who walked beside the donkey?
8. How far did they walk?
9. Name two things which they were doing besides walking.
10. How many people carried sticks?

The noun **man** is of the **Masculine** Gender. (he)
The noun **woman** is of the **Feminine** Gender. (she)
The noun **donkey** is of the **Common** Gender. (it)

15

Draw three columns with the headings shown, then place the nouns below in their proper columns.

Masculine   **Feminine**   **Common**

queen, orphan, witch, negro, cousin, nephew, bride, doctor, companion, sister, widow, bull, landlord, child, prince, aunt, student, actor, uncle, competitor

 Look at these two sentences:
Today I say "No". (Present Tense)
Yesterday I said "No". (Past Tense)

Now fill in the blanks below:

Today	Yesterday		Today	Yesterday
1. I break	I ——	6. I drink	I ——
2. I am	I ——	7. I think	I ——
3. I bite	I ——	8. I give	I ——
4. I buy	I ——	9. I go	I ——
5. I know	I ——	10. I sleep	I ——

 Nouns are the names of things.
Examples: dog, book, window, cloud

Verbs are words which express actions.
Examples: listen, hear, sing, loiter

Adjectives are words which describe nouns.
Examples: beautiful, horrible, wealthy, glad

Now arrange these words from the extract in three columns, under the headings shown.

Nouns		**Adjectives**		**Verbs**
appeared	rough	donkey	said	point
strong	lane	escorted	urchin	rapid
patted	tall	seemed	first	plan
horrible	set	nightmare	woman	object

16

E The word urchin which appeared in the passage from *The Mill On The Floss* means—a poor, ragged boy.

Which words can be used for these boys?

1. A boy whose parents are dead.

2. A boy who is cruel to those smaller than himself.

3. A boy who eats more than is good for him.

4. A boy who rescues his friend from drowning.

5. A boy who runs errands in a hotel.

F Each of the questions below contains clues to a pair of words which are pronounced alike but spelt differently. Write the ten pairs of words. (*Homonyms*)

Example: Question 1. (a) **beach** (b) **beech**

1. (a) part of the seashore
   (b) an English tree which bears nuts

2. (a) two things which go together
   (b) a common fruit

3. (a) a wooden frame to join oxen together
   (b) the yellow part of an egg

4. (a) a small dried fruit used in cakes and buns
   (b) a flow of water, air, electricity, etc.

5. (a) a blossom
   (b) the meal obtained by grinding wheat

6. (a) a flat stretch of land
   (b) a tool with a blade for smoothing wood

7. (a) a big gun which fires shells
   (b) a clergyman who is a member of a cathedral chapter

8. (a) a large bundle of raw cotton, wool, etc.
   (b) one of the cross pieces over the stumps in cricket

9. (a) the softer part inside the shell of a nut
   (b) an officer who commands a regiment

10. (a) grain food, like wheat, barley, oats, etc.
    (b) a story published in instalments, or a film shown one
        episode at a time

 G   Write about 15 lines on any one of these subjects.

      1. Gardening
      2. The Uses Of Trees
      3. A Car Journey I Enjoyed

Comprehension

HURRICANE

The boys were surprised to find our ostrich swallowing small pebbles, but I explained that the ostrich requires these to enable it to digest its food, just as fowls and most small birds need gravel.

"Hurricane", as Jack had named it, lived chiefly on vegetables, maize, and acorns, and became so tame that we could do as we liked with it. In less than a month it had been trained by Jack to walk and run with himself on its back, and to sit down, get up, and gallop at command.

A saddle was made and placed near the neck of the ostrich, partly resting on the shoulders and partly on the back, being fastened by a girth under the wings and across the breast. This position was necessary as the slope of the back would have rendered it unsafe, and the shoulders are the strongest part of a bird's back.

We did not expect Hurricane to act as a beast of burden, but as a fleet courser, and with Jack as its rider its journeys between Falcon's Nest and Rock Castle were performed with astonishing rapidity.

The Swiss Family Robinson by J. R. Wyss

1. Why did the ostrich swallow pebbles?

2. What name had Jack given to the ostrich?

3. What do fowls and most small birds swallow instead of pebbles?

4. What food did the ostrich eat?

5. How long did Jack take to tame the ostrich sufficiently to be ridden?

6. Where was the saddle of the ostrich placed?

19

7. How was it secured to the ostrich?

8. Why was the saddle placed in this position?

9. What was the ostrich used for?

10. Did it do its work well?

B The noun **rapidity** in the above passage has been formed from the adjective **rapid**. Form nouns from the following adjectives.

1. happy	6. deep
2. broad	7. high
3. popular	8. gallant
4. brave	9. ignorant
5. impudent	10. responsible

C In the above passage the plural of **journey** is used. Write the plurals of the following nouns which end with the letter **y**.

1. injury	6. chimney
2. pulley	7. remedy
3. story	8. bully
4. storey	9. hobby
5. canary	10. turkey

D In each of the sentences below you will see an underlined word with missing letters. Read the sentences carefully, then write the complete words in a column numbered 1 to 10.

1. The second month of the year is F b ___ y.

2. Jane has worn a d f r t frock every day this week.

3. The comedian entertained his guests with several h m r   s stories.

4. A serious accident oc   r d at the crossroads last night.

5. The G v   m   t decided to increase Retirement Pensions.

6. The Education C m   t e met to appoint a new headmaster.

7. "Treasure Island" is my f v   r   e book.

8. It is an ex   l   t story about pirates.

9. From the top of the hill we had a m   v   l   s view of the bay.

10. David has been taken to hospital for an op r   n.

E Read each sentence carefully before answering the question.

1. Jim wished that Tom's new bicycle was his.
> Which of these words describes Jim?
> generous, optimistic, dubious, envious

2. Pat Doolan was always ready for a fight.
> Write the word which describes Pat Doolan.
> artful, skilful, pugnacious, vicious

3. *Treasure Island* is not a true story.
> Which word describes *Treasure Island*?
> malicious, fictitious, humorous, continuous

4. John was unwilling to join the boys.
> Choose the word which describes John.
> reluctant, arrogant, triumphant, indignant

5. The leper's face was covered with sores.
> Write the word which describes the leper's face.
> impulsive, primitive, repulsive, destructive

21

F Write the missing words.

1. The lost explorers were almost dying of hunger and ——.

2. He will move heaven and —— to achieve his object.

3. It is natural that he should favour his own flesh and ——.

4. This book contains some beautiful selections of prose and ——.

5. I gave the beggar five pence because he looked down and ——.

G Write a composition of about 15 lines on any one of these subjects.

1. A Children's Playground
2. Animals I Like
3. A Story I Enjoyed.

22

TEST 5

Comprehension

FATHER WILLIAM

"You are old, Father William," the young man said,
   "And your hair has become very white;
And yet you incessantly stand on your head—
   Do you think, at your age, it is right?"

"In my youth," Father William replied to his son,
   "I feared I might injure the brain;
But now that I'm perfectly sure I have none,
   Why, I do it again and again."

"You are old," said the youth, "as I mentioned before,
   And have grown most uncommonly fat;
Yet you turned a back-somersault in at the door—
   Pray, what is the reason for that?"

"In my youth," said the sage, as he shook his grey locks,
   "I kept all my limbs very supple
By the use of this ointment—one shilling the box—
   Allow me to sell you a couple."

Alice's Adventures in Wonderland by Lewis Carroll

1. Why was Father William afraid to stand on his head when he was young?
2. Why was he not afraid to stand on his head in his old age?
3. How did Father William keep his limbs supple in his youth?
4. What did Father William do when he came in at the door?
5. Write the two adjectives which are used to describe the colour of Father William's hair.

6. What did Father William want to sell?
7. What would these have cost?
8. What is a "sage"?
9. Which word in the poem means "without stopping; continually"?
10. To whom was Father William speaking?

B Complete each of these sentences by inserting an adjective which begins with the letters **sh—**.

1. As it was so hot we sat down to rest beneath some tall sh—— trees.
2. Although the man's clothes were very sh—— he spoke politely to mother.
3. At the farm we were met by a dog with a sh—— coat.
4. The river was so sh—— at one place that we were able to wade across.
5. In a sh—— voice the farmer's wife ordered the boys to get out of the hayfield.

C Match the words in Column A with those in Column B.
Example: 1. teacher — pupil

Column A	Column B
1. teacher	patient
2. shopkeeper	servant
3. queen	tenant
4. doctor	pupil
5. lawyer	guest
6. parent	customer
7. husband	client
8. landlord	child
9. host	subject
10. master	wife

24

From the noun **burglar** we form the abstract noun **burglary.** Form abstract nouns from the following nouns by adding —**y,** —**ism,** —**hood,** —**ship,** etc.

1. man		6. tyrant
2. friend		7. hero
3. coward		8. infant
4. enemy		9. lunatic
5. glutton		10. rogue

 Write the names of the creatures which make the following sounds.

1. bleating		6. braying
2. hissing		7. howling
3. roaring		8. croaking
4. squeaking		9. squealing
5. hooting		10. trumpeting

Select one of the two words in brackets at the end of each sentence to complete the sentence correctly.

1. Gerard crept out on to the —— of the tree. (bow, bough)

2. Most people long for a lasting ——. (piece, peace)

3. The house is to be built on a perfectly flat ——. (site, sight)

4. The explorers were confronted by a —— of savages. (horde, hoard)

5. The cyclist found that his front —— was out of order. (break, brake)

6. A —— is a shellfish with a shell in two parts. (mussel, muscle)

7. A —— is a sleeping place on a ship, train or plane. (birth, berth)

8. On seeing the dog the rabbit bolted for its ——. (burrow, borough)

9. —— for the defence was a brilliant lawyer. (Counsel, Council)

10. We watched a young sailor trying to —— a boat across the harbour. (skull, scull)

G Write a composition of about 15 lines on any one of the following subjects.

1. Great Inventions
2. A Cricket Match I Watched
3. At The Fair

Comprehension

THE HORSE FAIR

Or course, I judged the buyers by their manners to myself. There was one man of whom I thought that if he would buy me I should be happy. He was a rather small man, and quick in all his motions. I knew in a moment by the way he handled me that he was used to horses; he spoke gently, and his grey eyes had a kindly, cheery look. The clean, fresh smell there was about him made me take to him. He offered twenty-three pounds for me; but that was refused, and he walked away.

A very hard-looking, loud-voiced man came next, and offered twenty-three pounds. A close bargain was being driven, for my salesman began to think he should not get all he asked, and must come down; but just then the grey-eyed man returned. I could not help reaching my head towards him, and he stroked my face kindly.

"Well, old chap," he said, "I think we should suit each other. I'll give twenty-four for him."

"Say twenty-five and you shall have him."

"Twenty-four ten," said my friend, in a very decided tone, "and not another sixpence—yes or no?"

"Done," said the salesman, and the money was paid on the spot.

My new master took my halter and led me out of the fair to an inn, where he had a saddle and a bridle ready. He gave me a good feed of oats, and stood by whilst I ate it, talking to himself and talking to me. Half an hour later we were on our way to London, which we reached at twilight.

Black Beauty by Anna Sewell

1. How did Black Beauty know that the small man was used to horses?

2. Why was Black Beauty attracted to this man?
3. How much did this man offer for Black Beauty at first?
4. What did he do when this offer was refused?
5. What did Black Beauty do to the grey-eyed man when he returned?
6. How did the man respond to this?
7. How much was Black Beauty eventually sold for?
8. Where was Black Beauty taken after he had been bought?
9. What was he given to eat?
10. How had Black Beauty's buyer prepared for the ride to London?

B Write the words ending with —**ment** which are needed to complete these sentences.

1. Mother liked the photograph so much that she is having an ——ment of it made.
2. The accused was sentenced to three months' ——ment.
3. Mr Robinson lost his job last month and is still out of ——ment.
4. The boxer received severe ——ment before he was finally knocked out.
5. The injured puppy was taken to the vet for ——ment.

 C Answer these questions on abbreviations.

1. On a bill appear the words Dr to John Strong, Grocer. Write the word which has been shortened to Dr.
2. What do the letters B.R. on a train stand for?
3. Your history book tells you that Julius Caesar landed in Britain in 55 B.C. What do the letters B.C. mean?

4. What do the letters P.C. stand for when written before a man's name?

5. What do the letters J.P. after a man's name signify?

 Change the following sentences into Direct Speech.

Example: Harry said that he would lock the door.
"I will lock the door," said Harry.

1. Susan asked Ann if she was going for a walk.
2. Mrs Maggs told the butcher that the pork he sent her the previous day was too fat.
3. Mother complained that she had a pain in her back.
4. David's teacher told him that he should always check his sums.
5. Mary said that she was too tired to watch television.

E One word in each sentence below is misspelt. Replace it with a word which has the same sound, but a different spelling.

1. The car took the shortest root to Bristol.
2. The bride walked gracefully down the isle.
3. The weather vein showed that the wind was blowing from the north.
4. To ensure that walls are built upright builders use a plum line.
5. The prisoner admitted his gilt.
6. In crossing the style Jane slipped and tore her frock.
7. Mother put too much time in the stuffing.
8. At the wedding breakfast there was a lovely three tear cake.
9. In eastern countries many women wear a vale.
10. For lunch we had place and chips.

Complete the words in the squares below, using one letter in each square.

		e	a			=	perspiration
		e	a			=	a bundle of corn, wheat, etc.
		e	a			=	inexpensive
		e	a			=	another word for pilfer
		e	a			=	"the staff of life"

 Write a composition of about 15 lines on any one of the following subjects.

1. My Hobby
2. A Church I Have Visited
3. Ships

Comprehension

THE ARTFUL DODGER

The Artful Dodger took Oliver to a nearby shop, where he bought a quantity of boiled ham and a fourpenny loaf, the ham being kept clean by making a hole in the loaf, by pulling out a portion of the crumb, and stuffing it therein. Taking the bread under his arm the young gentleman turned into a small public-house, and led the way to a taproom at the rear of the premises. Here a pot of beer was brought in, by the directions of the mysterious youth; and Oliver, falling to at his new friend's bidding, made a long and hearty meal, during the progress of which the strange boy eyed him from time to time with great attention.

"Going to London?" asked the strange boy, when Oliver had concluded.

"Yes."

"Got any lodgings?"

"No."

"Money?"

"No."

The strange boy whistled and put his arms into his pockets as far as the big sleeves would let them go.

"Do you live in London?" inquired Oliver.

"Yes, I do when I'm at home," replied the Artful Dodger. "I suppose you want some place to sleep in tonight, don't you?"

"I do indeed," answered Oliver. "I have not slept under a roof since I left the country."

Oliver Twist by Charles Dickens

1. What did the Artful Dodger buy in the shop?
2. To what part of the public-house did the Dodger take Oliver?

3. Where was this situated?
4. How was the ham kept clean?
5. Who ordered the pot of beer?
6. What was the Dodger doing whilst Oliver was eating his meal?
7. What was Oliver's destination?
8. Where did the Dodger live?
9. Where had Oliver been sleeping since leaving the country?
10. Write three adjectives used to describe the Dodger.

B The word **vegetable** is a class name, and includes potatoes, cabbages, turnips, carrots, etc. Write the class name for each of the following groups.

1. carnation, snowdrop, tulip, daffodil
2. red, blue, yellow, green
3. iron, lead, copper, aluminium
4. motor-car, bus, taxi, caravan
5. Europe, Asia, Africa, America, Australia

C Write the opposites of the words in heavy type in these sentences.

1. An abundant **supply** of fish was landed, but the —— for it was small.
2. We turned from the **broad** avenue into a —— lane.
3. The number of births **increased** by 125, and the number of deaths —— by 98.
4. An accused person is considered **innocent** until he is proved ——.
5. **Wise** people provide for their future, but —— people leave things to chance.

D Rewrite the following phrases so as to include the apostrophe (').

Examples: the trunk of the elephant
the elephant's trunk

the trunks of the elephants
the elephants' trunks

1. the fur of the cat
2. the collar of the dog
3. the home for dogs
4. the den of the lion
5. the den of the lions
6. a short for a boy
7. a club for boys
8. a choir of men
9. the crown of the Queen
10. the webs of the spiders

E The missing words from these sentences all begin with the letter **p.** What are they?

1. The cobra is a deadly p—— snake.
2. The Flying Squad went in p—— of the thieves.
3. Joan doesn't play the piano well; she needs more p——.
4. Robert is making very good p—— in school.
5. The sergeant was p—— to the rank of inspector.
6. Many Welsh words are too difficult for English people to p——.
7. The centre-forward was p—— for handling the ball.
8. The p—— of London is about 8,000,000.
9. The firm allows a discount of 5p in the £ for p—— payment of bills.
10. It was so hot that the p—— streamed down our faces.

B

F Insert these ten words in their correct places in the joke which follows.

agree	cackle	matter	decided	whether
argued	unable	know	right	want

Two men ...(1)... as to ...(2)... it was right to say that a hen was "sitting" or "setting".

Being ...(3)... to ...(4)... they ...(5)... to ask Farmer Dale.

"Boys," he said, "it doesn't ...(6)... which is ...(7).... All I ...(8)... to ...(9)... when I hear a hen ...(10)... is whether she's 'laying' or 'lying'."

G Write a composition of about 15 lines on any one of the following subjects.

1. Walking In The Park
2. Ways Of Travelling
3. Christmas Preparations

34

Comprehension

A THRILLING ESCAPE

As his dying steed collapsed beneath him Dick Varley sprang up, for the Indians were now upon him, and bounded into the thickest part of the shrubbery, which was nowhere thick enough, however, to prevent the Indians following. Still, it sufficiently delayed them to make the chase a more equal one.

In a few minutes Dick gained a strip of open ground beyond, and found himself on the bank of a broad river, which was, at this spot, a sheer precipice of between thirty and forty feet high. Glancing up and down the river he retreated a few paces, turned round, and then, running to the edge of the bank, sprang far out into the boiling flood and sank.

The Indians pulled up on reaching the spot; and each Redskin leaped to the ground, and, fitting an arrow to his bow, awaited Dick's reappearance. Dick knew what sort of reception he would meet with on coming to the surface, so he kept under water as long as he could, and struck out as vigorously as the care of his rifle would permit. At last he rose for a few seconds, and immediately half a dozen arrows whizzed through the air, most of them falling short, but one passing close to his cheek. He immediately sank again, and the next time he rose to breathe he was far beyond the reach of his enemies.

The Dog Crusoe by R. M. Ballantyne

1. Where did Dick Varley make for when his horse collapsed?
2. Why did he make for this place?
3. What lay between this place and the bank of the river?
4. How high was the bank of the river at the spot where Dick reached it?
5. What did Dick do before leaping into the river?
6. What did the Indians do on reaching the river?

7. Why did Dick stay under water as long as he could?
8. What hampered his efforts to swim under water?
9. What happened when he rose to the surface the first time?
10. What did he find when he rose to the surface the second time?

 Fit these ten adjectives into their correct places in the phrases below.

intricate   impregnable   industrial   fruitless
opportune   vivid   furtive   ingenious
momentary   unquenchable

1. a —— glance
2. an —— idea
3. a —— pause
4. an —— fortress
5. an —— moment
6. a —— description
7. an —— problem
8. a —— search
9. an —— thirst
10. an —— town

C What are the collective nouns needed to complete the following sentences?

1. We have a new —— of furniture in the lounge.
2. A —— of bees buzzed round the picnickers' heads.
3. At the Whist Drive there was a new —— of playing cards on each table.
4. Huge —— of grapes hung from the vine.
5. The carpenter bought a new —— of tools to replace those he had lost.

 Complete these similes.

1. as busy as a ——
2. as cunning as a ——
3. as brown as a ——
4. as cool as a ——
5. as dead as a ——
6. as bold as ——
7. as hard as ——
8. as quick as ——
9. as safe as ——
10. as sweet as ——

36

E　　The first sentence in each of these pairs contains an idiom from which one word is missing. The second sentence explains the idiom. Write the missing words, numbering them 1 to 10.

1. Sally's heart was in her ——.
   (Sally was very frightened.)

2. We must strike while the —— is hot
   (We must act without delay.)

3. I think Dad smells a ——.
   (I think Dad has his suspicions.)

4. Peter is a —— of the old block.
   (Peter is exactly like his father.)

5. Harold was sent to —— by his classmates.
   (Harold was shunned by his classmates.)

6. Paul is fond of blowing his own ——.
   (Paul is fond of boasting.)

7. Private Johnson took —— leave.
   (Private Johnson was absent from camp without permission.)

8. Richard was hauled over the —— for his bad behaviour.
   (Richard was scolded and punished for his bad behaviour.)

9. Uncle Bob hit the —— on the head.
   (Uncle Bob was quite right.)

10. Everything is above ——.
    (Everything is perfectly straightforward.)

F　　Write the abbreviations for:

1. Mister	6. Limited
2. Reverend	7. Company
3. Esquire	8. Street
4. Doctor	9. Road
5. Number	10. Lieutenant

Write a composition of about 15 lines on any one of these subjects.

1. Work On A Farm
2. Town Or Country? Which Do You Prefer?
3. Camping Out

TEST 9

Comprehension

THE SHEPHERD

The shepherd, happily stretched beneath a hedge, was composing verses in praise of his love, sweetly singing them to the listening echoes, and then repeating the air on his flute.

The King was astonished, and said, "This beautiful flock will soon be destroyed; the wolves will scarcely be afraid of lovesick shepherds, singing to their shepherdesses; a flute is a sorry weapon wherewith to repel them. Oh! How I should laugh!—"

At this moment a wolf comes in sight; but scarcely has it appeared when a watchful dog springs upon it and throttles it. Two sheep, frightened at the noise of the combat, quit the flock and run about the plain. Another dog sets off, brings them back, and order is restored instantly. The shepherd views all without ceasing to play.

Hereupon the King said to him half angrily, "How do you manage? The woods are filled with wolves; your sheep, fat and beautiful, are almost countless; yet with the utmost ease you take care of the whole flock yourself!"

"Sire," replied the shepherd, "the thing is perfectly easy; my whole secret consists in making choice of good dogs."

Fables From Florian

1. Where was the shepherd lying?
2. Name three things that he was doing.
3. Why was the King astonished?
4. What did the King fear would happen?
5. What creature came into sight as the King was speaking to the shepherd?

6. What happened to this creature?
7. What effect did this have on two of the sheep?
8. What did the second dog do?
9. What was the shepherd doing whilst these things were happening?
10. Why was the shepherd able to take care of his large flock without exerting himself?

 B Complete each sentence below by inserting a collective noun beginning with the letter **b.**

1. John took the b—— of keys which he had found to the police station.
2. The Duchess was presented with a beautiful b—— of flowers.
3. As soon as one b—— of bread was taken out of the oven another was put in.
4. The dockers were glad when the last b—— of cotton was put on board.
5. In one corner of the tailor's workshop was a large b—— of rags.

C Insert the correct word in each sentence.

1. I couldn't write to Jennifer as I had no ——. (stationary, stationery)
2. Dad's driving —— expires this week. (licence, license)
3. The woman said she would —— my apologies. (except, accept)
4. The witness was cross-examined by the —— for the defence. (council, counsel)
5. The —— of the college praised the work of the students. (principal, principle)

D Complete each of the sentences below by inserting in the blank spaces the Past Tense of the verb in brackets at the end.

Example: Tom —— all the cake. (eat)
Answer: ate

1. Dad —— all the expenses of the holiday. (bear)
2. The champion —— the fight of his life. (fight)
3. Dick —— his football in lacing it with an awl. (burst)
4. I —— in bed all yesterday morning. (lie)
5. Ian —— when he said he had no money. (lie)
6. In tackling an opponent the full-back —— his knee. (hurt)
7. Mary —— the table for tea. (lay)
8. The defeated army —— in disorder. (flee)
9. Tom's pullover —— in the wash. (shrink)
10. The speaker —— very fully with the questions put to him. (deal)

E Use your knowledge of proverbs to answer these questions.

Example: Question: What is as good as a feast?
Answer: Enough

1. What will a drowning man clutch at?
2. What makes the heart grow fonder?
3. What is it that gathers no moss?
4. Where does charity begin?
5. What kind of vessels make most noise?
6. What kind of birds flock together?
7. What catches the worm?
8. What is the mother of invention?
9. What do new brooms do?
10. What should you do before you leap?

Write the opposites of the following verbs.

1. sold
2. advance
3. import
4. increase
5. expand

6. persuade
7. hurry
8. punish
9. conceal
10. create

Write a composition of about 15 lines on any one of the following subjects.

1. Collecting Postage Stamps
2. A Sea Story
3. Sounds I Like

TEST 10

Comprehension

BIRD FIGHTS

Ten sparrows came from the house-top into the bushes, chattering and struggling all together, and all talking at once. After they had had a good fight they all went back to the house-top, and began to tell each other what tremendous blows they had given.

Then there was such a great cawing from the rookery, which was a long way off, that it was evident a battle was going on there, and Bevis heard the chaffinch say that one of the rooks had been caught stealing his cousin's sticks.

Then a blackbird came up from the brook and perched on a rail, and he was such a boaster, for he said he had the yellowest bill of all the blackbirds, and the blackest coat, and the largest eyes, and the sweetest whistle. In two minutes up came another one from out of the bramble bushes at the corner, and away they went chattering at each other.

Presently the starlings on the chimney began to quarrel, and had a terrible set-to. Then a wren came by, and though he was so small his boast was worse than the blackbird's, for he said he was the sharpest and the cleverest of all the birds, and knew more than all put together.

Wood Magic by Richard Jefferies

1. Where did the fight between the sparrows take place?

2. Where did the sparrows fly to when the fight was over?

3. Why did fighting break out in the rookery?

4. Which of the birds knew why the rooks were fighting?

5. Name four things about which the first blackbird boasted.

6. Where did the second blackbird come from?

43

7. What happened when he met the first blackbird?
8. Where were the starlings quarrelling?
9. Which bird was the most boastful of all?
10. What did he boast about?

B Fill in the gaps with the names of the young of the creatures.

Example: The cat carried her —— in her mouth.
Answer: kittens

1. The cow was lowing loudly for its ——.
2. The polar bear was busy licking her ——.
3. The mother goose was very proud of her six fluffy ——.
4. In a field the children saw a nanny-goat with her two little ——.
5. The little —— hid under the mother hen's wings.

C Look carefully at the definition of each word in the column on the left, then write the complete word.

1. **bble   = a small round stone
2. **bble   = a disorderly crowd; a mob
3. ***bble = to move a football along the ground with short kicks
4. **bble   = to swallow food in big pieces
5. **bble   = rough broken bricks, stones, etc.
6. **bble   = to walk awkwardly; to limp
7. **bble   = to talk indistinctly, like a baby
8. **bble   = to move unsteadily from side to side
9. ***bble = a short, rough growth of beard
10. ***bble = to evade the truth by twisting the meaning of words

44

D Fill the spaces in these sentences by forming the correct noun from the verb in brackets.

Example: act — actor
preside — president

1. There was only one —— for the post. (apply)
2. The champion meets a clever —— tonight. (oppose)
3. The —— worked hard for the arithmetic examination. (study)
4. At the Horticultural Show one —— won nine prizes. (compete)
5. The —— was clapped in irons. (mutiny)

E Fill the gap in each sentence below by using the Participle of the verb in brackets.

Example: The champion was —— on points. (beat)
Answer: beaten

1. Mary was —— to be Carnival Queen. (choose)
2. Dick's elbow was badly —— after the accident. (swell)
3. After Jack had —— in bed for a few hours he felt much better. (lie)
4. Mother discovered that the children had —— all her sweets. (eat)
5. The door of the cage was open; the bird had ——. (fly)
6. Several bathers were —— during the summer holidays. (drown)
7. The football has ——, so we cannot play. (burst)
8. Many of the papers had been —— underfoot. (tread)
9. The Marines, who had —— the brunt of the fighting, were completely exhausted. (bear)
10. The pearls were —— behind a picture. (hide)

F Arrange the following adjectives in two columns, under these headings:

Large   **Small**

vast, colossal, minute, diminutive, immense
tiny, mammoth, enormous, miniature, microscopic

G Write a composition of about 15 lines on any one of these subjects.

1. How Our School Could Be Improved
2. Modern Aircraft
3. Puppet Shows

TEST 11

Comprehension

RIP VAN WINKLE

As Rip Van Winkle was about to descend the mountain he heard a voice from the distance calling his name, and presently saw a strange figure slowly toiling up the rocks, bending under the weight of something he carried on his back. He was a short, square-built old fellow, and his dress was of the antique Dutch fashion. On his shoulder he carried a stout keg that seemed full of liquor, and he made signs to Rip to approach him and assist him with the load. Rip complied, and they clambered up the narrow gully in silence. As they ascended Rip heard long rolling peals like distant thunder.

Presently they arrived at a level spot, in the centre of which was a company of odd-looking persons playing nine-pins. Whenever the balls were rolled the noise echoed along the mountains like peals of thunder.

As Rip and his companion approached them they stopped their play and stared at him. His companion now emptied the contents of the keg into large flagons and made signs to Rip to wait upon the company. He obeyed, and they drank the liquor in silence, then returned to their game.

Being a naturally thirsty soul, Rip was tempted to taste the beverage, and finding it to his liking took another drink and another until at last his senses were overpowered, and he fell into a deep sleep, from which he did not awake for twenty years.

Rip Van Winkle by Washington Irving

1. What did Rip hear as he was about to descend?
2. How was the stranger dressed?
3. What did the stranger carry on his shoulder?
4. What did the stranger want Rip to do?
5. Did Rip oblige him?

6. What did Rip hear as he ascended the gully?
7. What caused this noise?
8. What did the odd-looking persons do as Rip approached?
9. What did Rip's companion do with the liquor?
10. State fully the effect the liquor had on Rip.

B Complete each of the following sentences by inserting the adjective formed from the noun in brackets.

Example: Switzerland is a —— country. (mountain)
Answer: mountainous

1. The blacksmith rolled up his sleeves, exposing his —— arms. (muscle)
2. The survivors were —— to escape with slight injuries. (fortune)
3. The policeman on duty gave the Prime Minister his —— salute. (custom)
4. The —— boxer was cheered from the ring. (victory)
5. A poor, —— boy was begging in the street. (rag)
6. It is an advantage to have —— friends. (influence)
7. We should always avoid —— methods in arithmetic. (labour)
8. The —— monkey snatched Peter's spectacles and broke them. (mischief)
9. James is a —— boy. (quarrel)
10. The football team was led by a —— captain. (youth)

C Complete these proverbs:

1. A friend in need ....
2. Better late ....
3. First come ....
4. It's an ill wind.....................
5. An apple a day ....

48

D Fit the ten adverbs below into the blank spaces in the sentences.

cordially   grudgingly
unanimously   contemptuously
insolently   candidly
familiarly   frugally
obstinately   luxuriously

1. The doctor told his patient quite —— what he thought of his behaviour.

2. —— the miser handed the beggar a halfpenny.

3. The strikers decided —— to resume work.

4. The lounge was —— furnished.

5. With a weekly income of only £15 the widow was compelled to live ——.

6. The mutineer glared —— at the captain.

7. The foreign visitors were —— welcomed by the Mayor.

8. Williams was —— known to the boys of Rugby School as "The Slogger".

9. The mule —— refused to cross the footbridge.

10. The countess looked —— at the grovelling servant.

E Select the correct definition (a), (b), or (c) for each of the adjectives in capital letters. Each answer consists of a number and a letter.

1. A **unique** article is:
    (a) brand new
    (b) extremely valuable
    (c) the only one in existence

2. **Consecutive** numbers are:
    (a) successive numbers like 7, 8, 9, 10, etc.
    (b) those which have factors, like 12, 15, etc.
    (c) those which have no factors, like 13, 17, 19, etc.

3. A **bashful** boy is:
    (a) very shy
    (b) a bully and a coward
    (c) quite at ease in the company of others

4. A **hospitable** person:
    (a) is unfriendly towards others
    (b) gives a warm welcome to visitors
    (c) nurses people who are seriously ill

5. A **versatile** person is one who:
    (a) can do many things well
    (b) can recite poetry fluently
    (c) is skilled in repairing roofs

F Rewrite these sentences correctly.

1. Dad bought a Christmas tree from a nurseryman three metres high.
2. A bottle was lost by a doctor containing dangerous drugs.
3. In the workshop we saw a carpenter sawing timber with a wooden leg.
4. David invited me to go hiking with him in a long letter.
5. A cowman was milking a red cow in dungarees.

G Write a composition of about 15 lines on any one of the following subjects.

1. My Pet
2. The House I Live In
3. Songs I Like

50

Comprehension

THE HOVEL

Near the north end of Deal beach there stood an upturned boat, which served its owner as a hut or shelter from which he could sit and scan the sea. This hut, or hovel, was a roomy and snug enough place even in rough weather, and although intended chiefly as a place of outlook, it nevertheless had various conveniences which made it little short of a veritable habitation.

Among these were a small stove and a swinging oil-lamp which, when lighted, filled the interior with a ruddy glow that quite warmed one to look at. A low door at one end of the hovel faced the sea, and there was a small square hole or window beside it through which the end of a telescope generally protruded, for the occupants of the hut spent most of their idle time in taking observations of the sea. There was a bench on either side of the hovel which was lumbered with a confused mass of spars, sails, sou'-westers, oilskin coats and trousers, buoys, sea-chests, rudders, tar-barrels and telescopes.

The Lifeboat by R. M. Ballantyne

1. At which end of Deal beach did the hovel stand?
2. What was the boat used for?
3. How was the hovel heated?
4. How was it lighted?
5. In which direction did the door face?
6. Where was the small square hole?
7. What was it used for?
8. How did the occupants of the hut spend most of their spare time?
9. How many benches were there in the hovel?
10. Name three articles of sailors' clothing which lumbered the hut.

B The word **habitation** in the above passage means a dwelling, a place to live in. The missing words in the following sentences are the names of dwellings. What are they?

1. The convict felt very miserable sitting alone in his ——.
2. The vicar complained that the —— had more rooms than he could afford to furnish.
3. There are thirty-five monks living in the ——.
4. The Eskimos were building a new —— with blocks of frozen snow.
5. The Bishop's —— was a very large building situated in spacious grounds.

C You read in the above passage that the boat served its owner as a hut. The word **its** means **belongs to it.** Write the missing words in these sentences.

1. This ball is ——. (belonging to me)
2. Michael said that book is ——. (belonging to him)
3. These apples are ——. (belonging to us)
4. Are these clothes ——? (belonging to you)
5. The girls claimed that the tennis rackets were ——. (belonging to them)

D Rewrite these sentences, using one word in place of those in heavy type.

1. The little toy soldier was **covered with rust.**
2. Most of the survivors were **natives of Poland.**
3. Tom's teacher considers him **a child who is very slow at learning.**
4. The police **took the weapons from** the gunmen.

5. Hundreds of people were **without food and shelter** after the earthquake.

E Join each pair of sentences together to make a longer sentence.

Example: Jack slept late. He lost the school bus.
Jack slept late and lost the school bus.

1. Guy Fawkes was charged with treason. He was condemned to death.
2. Finney sent in a terrific shot. It crashed against the crossbar.
3. The shops were closed. We could get nothing to eat.
4. Mother was very worried. She had lost a £10 note.
5. We waited till the end of Compton's innings. We went home.

F The opposites of many adjectives are formed by writing **un, il, in, im, ir, dis,** or **non** before them.

Examples: tidy — untidy
honest — dishonest

Write the opposite of each adjective in heavy type in these sentences.
1. Freda is a very **attractive** girl.
2. At the restaurant our order was taken by a **courteous** waiter.
3. Mary wore an **expensive** wrap over her frock.
4. Some of the clerks were doing **essential** work.
5. The analyst found that the well water was **pure.**
6. James is a most **responsible** boy.
7. On the table were several kinds of **intoxicating** drinks.
8. The business transacted by the firm was quite **legal.**

53

9. Most of the doctor's friends were **loyal** during his trial.

10. The repairs to our car were carried out by an **efficient** mechanic.

G Write a composition of about 15 lines on any one of the following.

   1. Personal Cleanliness
   2. A Holiday I Would Like
   3. Our School

TEST 13

Comprehension

TRADING WITH ESKIMOS

First of all, several presents were made to the Eskimos, who were overjoyed at receiving such trifles as bits of hoop-iron, beads, knives, scissors, needles, etc. Iron is as precious among them as gold is among civilised people. The small quantities they possessed had been obtained from the few portions of wrecks that had drifted ashore on their ice-bound land. They used the iron for pointing their spear-heads and harpoons, which, when they were without iron, they made of ivory from the tusks of the walrus. A bit of iron, therefore, was received with immense glee, and a penny looking-glass with shouts of delight.

But the present which drew forth the most uproarious applause was a Union Jack, which the captain gave to their chief, Awatok. He was in the cabin when it was presented to him. On seeing its gaudy colours unrolled, and being told that it was a gift to himself and his wife, he gave vent to a tremendous shout, seized the flag, hugged it in his arms, and darted up on deck roaring with delight.

The skins and boots, besides walrus and seal-flesh, which the crew were enabled to barter at this time were of the utmost importance, for their fresh provisions had begun to get low, and their boots were almost worn out.

The World of Ice by R. M. Ballantyne

1. What was the name of the chief of the Eskimos?

2. Which of the presents did the Eskimos prize most?

3. Where did they usually get this substance from?

4. What did they use this substance for?

5. When this substance was unobtainable what did they use instead?

55

6. What present did the captain give to the Eskimo chief?
7. Where did the presentation take place?
8. What did the chief do when he got this present?
9. What did the crew get from the Eskimos in exchange for the goods they had given them?
10. Why was it important that they should get these things?

B Insert **past** or **passed**, as required, in the spaces in these sentences.

1. With a swerve Georgie Best raced —— the full-back and —— the ball to the centre forward.
2. As I —— the old mill a dark figure brushed —— me.
3. It was ten minutes —— five when we —— the town clock.
4. John —— his aunt's house without stopping to tell her that he had —— his examination.
5. Wilfred reached —— Ann as he —— the cakes to Margaret.

C In each line select the word which is nearest in meaning to the word in heavy type.

1. **expensive:** cheap, durable, costly, extensive
2. **renowned:** generous, celebrated, detested, evil
3. **infirm:** sturdy, patient, anxious, feeble
4. **eternal:** everlasting, external, temporary, lovely
5. **immediately:** presently, recently, instantly, steadily

D Who were the authors of these books?

1. Oliver Twist
2. Robinson Crusoe
3. Treasure Island
4. Alice in Wonderland
5. Little Women
6. Lorna Doone
7. Tom Brown's Schooldays
8. The Coral Island
9. Pilgrim's Progress
10. Black Beauty

E   In each of the following sentences the verb, which begins with the letter **d,** has been left out. Write the ten verbs.

1. The children were caught in the heavy rain and were d—— to the skin.
2. Lawrence d—— having broken the vase.
3. Grandpa is sleeping; don't d—— him.
4. The coal was d—— to the school in an articulated lorry.
5. Christopher Columbus d—— America in 1492.
6. The ship, disabled by the storm, d—— helplessly towards the rocky coast.
7. Thousands of buildings were completely d—— by the Great Fire of London.
8. The detective was d—— as a gipsy.
9. Several old buildings were d—— to make room for the new houses.
10. The manager d—— a letter to his secretary, who took it down in shorthand.

F   Complete each sentence by inserting the noun which corresponds to the adjective in brackets.

Example: We were charmed by the —— of the scenery. (grand)
Answer: grandeur

1. It was a time of great —— for the lost child's parents. (anxious)
2. The rose is noted for its ——. (fragrant)
3. In arithmetic the aim should be ——. (accurate)
4. The corporal was praised for his ——. (gallant)
5. Sarah was unpopular because of her ——. (vain)

G   Write a composition of about 15 lines on any one of subjects.

            1. Newspapers
            2. A Brave Deed
            3. Foods I Enjoy

TEST 14

Comprehension

WHITEWASHING

Tom appeared on the side-walk with a bucket of whitewash and a long-handled brush. He surveyed the fence which his Aunt Polly had ordered him to whitewash as a punishment for being naughty, and the gladness went out of his nature.

Thirty yards of broad fence nine feet high! It seemed to him that life was hollow, and existence but a burden. Sighing, he dipped his brush into the whitewash and passed it along the topmost plank; repeated the operation; did it again; compared the insignificant whitewashed streak with the far-reaching continent of unwhitewashed fence, and sat down on a tree-box discouraged. Jim came skipping out at the gate with a tin pail, and singing "Buffalo Gals". Bringing water from the town pump had always been hateful work in Tom's eyes before, but now it did not strike him so. He remembered that there was company at the pump. White, and negro boys and girls were always there waiting their turns, resting, trading playthings, quarrelling, fighting, skylarking. And he remembered that although the pump was only a hundred and fifty yards off Jim never got back with a bucket of water under an hour; and even then somebody generally had to go after him.

The Adventures of Tom Sawyer by Mark Twain

1. Why was Tom whitewashing the fence?

2. What was he carrying as he appeared on the side-walk?

3. How many square yards of fence did Tom have to whitewash?

4. Which part of the fence did Tom start whitewashing?

5. What did he do after making a few strokes with the brush?

6. What was Jim carrying as he came out at the gate?

7. How far away was the town pump?

8. Name five ways in which the children passed the time whilst waiting their turn at the pump.
9. How long did Jim usually take to fetch a bucket of water?
10. What happened when Jim lingered at the town pump?

B Complete each sentence below by inserting the adverb formed from the word in brackets.

Example: The farmer shouted —— at the boys in his hayfield.
  (angry)
Answer: angrily

1. The mirror was —— broken. (accidental)
2. The work had been done ——. (satisfactory)
3. Although outnumbered the Guards fought ——. (heroic)
4. Oliver Twist gazed —— at the bread and gruel. (hungry)
5. The burglar climbed —— through the open window. (stealthy)

C Here are ten verbs which begin with **re—**. Use one of these verbs in place of the verb in heavy type in each sentence below.

| resided | resolved | requested | released | responded |
| refused | retained | resisted | resumed | recollected |

1. Several prisoners-of-war were **liberated.**
2. The committee **declined** to consider the matter.
3. Mr Linto has **lived** in the district for several years.
4. After a brief interval the discussion was **continued.**
5. A large number of people **answered** to the call for blood donors.
6. The sea-wall has **withstood** the storms for many years.
7. Jimmy **determined** to do better at the next examination.
8. Sir Robert **kept** his seat at yesterday's election.
9. The chairman **asked** the committee to be seated.
10. Henry suddenly **remembered** where he had put his season ticket.

D The missing verb in each of the following sentences is formed from the noun in brackets.

1. Trees help to —— the streets of our towns. (beauty)
2. The kind lady promised to —— the little orphans. (friend)
3. Settlers in foreign countries often have to —— themselves to the climate. (custom)
4. The children continued to —— over the loss of their kitten. (grief)
5. A ship's captain should not —— the lives of his passengers. (danger)
6. Careless motorists —— the lives of pedestrians. (peril)
7. The nation has been requested to —— with coal. (economy)
8. The sale was an attempt to —— the public. (fraud)
9. The motorist's injuries will —— an operation. (necessity)
10. All children should —— the multiplication tables. (memory)

E Here are ten verbs numbered 1 to 10 and ten meanings lettered (a) to (j). Write the numbers 1 to 10 in a column, and opposite each write the letter which indicates the correct meaning.

Verbs	Meanings
1. postpone	(a) to seek information or advice from
2. distribute	(b) to scorn; to look down on
3. lament	(c) to seize property by authority
4. consult	(d) to annoy; to make angry
5. omit	(e) to pull apart; to take to pieces
6. disdain	(f) to put off till later
7. ponder	(g) to divide and give out in shares
8. confiscate	(h) to express grief; to mourn
9. irritate	(i) to consider carefully
10. dismantle	(j) to leave out

F Write the opposites of the following words. Every opposite should begin with the letter **s**.

1. plentiful
2. deep
3. fresh
4. rough
5. blunt

6. tight
7. crooked
8. plural
9. failure
10. inferior

G Write a composition of about 15 lines on any one of the following subjects.

1. Sounds Which Annoy Me
2. A Dream I Had
3. Electricity In The Home

A

Comprehension

TOM AND THE KEEPER

Tom descended from the tree in which he had hidden and wended his way drearily by the side of the keeper up to the Schoolhouse, where they arrived just at locking-up. As they passed the School gates the Tadpole and several others who were standing there caught the state of things and rushed out, crying "Rescue!" but Tom shook his head, so they only followed to the Doctor's gate, and went back sorely puzzled.

How changed and stern the Doctor seemed from the last time that Tom was up there, as the keeper told the story, not omitting to state how Tom had called him blackguard names.

"Indeed, sir," broke in the culprit, "it was only Velveteens." The Doctor only asked one question.

"You know that you are not allowed to fish from the bank opposite the School, Brown?"

"Yes, sir,"

"Then wait for me tomorrow, after first lesson."

"I thought so," muttered Tom.

"And about the rod, sir," went on the keeper. "Master's told us as we might have all the rods—"

"Oh, please, sir," broke in Tom, "the rod isn't mine."

The Doctor looked puzzled, but the keeper, who was a goodhearted fellow, and melted at Tom's evident distress, gave up his claim. Tom was flogged next morning, and a few days afterwards met Velveteens, and presented him with half-a-crown for giving up the rod claim, and they became sworn friends, and Tom had many more fish that season, but was never caught again by Velveteens.

Tom Brown's Schooldays by Thomas Hughes

1. Who stood outside the School gates as Tom and the keeper arrived?

2. What did they intend doing?
3. Why did they not carry out their intentions?
4. What did the keeper not forget to tell the Doctor?
5. What rule had Tom broken?
6. What claim did the keeper make?
7. Why did he make this claim?
8. Why did he not press his claim?
9. How did Tom reward him for giving up his claim?
10. In what way was Tom punished for his offence?

B A **Common Noun** is used for any one of a class.
    Examples: boy; dog; country

A **Proper Noun** is used to name one particular person, thing or place.
    Examples: Jack; Carlo; Belgium

A Proper Noun always begins with a capital letter.

Write the Proper Nouns contained in these sentences.

1. It was dusk before oliver reached london.
2. We visited nelson's ship, the victory.
3. The capital of holland is amsterdam.
4. Two men crossed the pacific ocean in a small boat.
5. We sent invitations to fred and betty.
6. About the middle of january harry was taken ill.
7. Huge crowds gathered round buckingham palace.
8. The roundheads were led by cromwell.
9. We saw the film of shakespeare's play hamlet.
10. I go away every easter and christmas.

C Insert in the blank space in each sentence below the adjective which corresponds to the verb.

Example: A —— result is one which satisfies.
Answer: satisfactory

1. A —— motor-car is one on which you can rely.
2. A —— task is one you are compelled to do.

63

3. A —— person meddles in other people's affairs.
4. An —— child observes what is going on around him.
5. A —— cough is one which troubles you.
6. An —— person envies others.
7. A —— child likes destroying things.
8. A —— battle decides the outcome of a war.
9. A —— amount is so small that it can be neglected.
10. A —— canoe is one that can be collapsed for easy storage.

D The missing words in these sentences are the names of famous characters from literature.

1. —— —— and his Merry Men lived in Sherwood Forest.
2. Giant —— lived in Doubting Castle.
3. —— taught Oliver Twist and other boys to pick pockets.
4. Mr —— was the brutal, ignorant headmaster of Dotheboys Hall.
5. —— —— rode from London to York on his mare Black Bess.

E The missing words in these sentences are all names of parts of the body.

1. To have a swelled —— means to be very conceited.
2. To pay through the —— for something means to pay an excessive price.
3. To throw dust in a person's —— means to deceive him.
4. To keep a stiff upper —— means to be brave in the face of danger or difficulties.
5. To make a clean —— of it means to make a full confession.
6. To be down in the —— means to be in low spirits; to be depressed.
7. To escape by the skin of one's —— means to have a very narrow escape.

64

8. To pull a person's —— means to deceive him in a humorous way; to hoax him.

9. To put one's best —— forward means to do one's very best.

10. To cut off your nose to spite your —— means to act in such a way as to injure yourself.

F What is the occupation of the person who sells:

1. cabbages, parsnips, carrots, leeks, onions, etc.
2. roses, carnations, wreaths, bouquets, sprays, etc.
3. hake, cod, herrings, mackerel, plaice, etc.
4. apples, pears, bananas, oranges, nuts, etc.
5. screws, nails, tools, hinges, nuts and bolts, etc.

G Write a composition of about 15 lines on any one of the following subjects.

1. My Home Town
2. A Fable I Like
3. Sport in Summer

C

65

TEST 16

Comprehension

THE GIANT ROC

One day we landed on an island, and while my companions were gathering flowers and fruits I took my wine and provisions and made a good meal near a stream between two high trees, which formed a thick shade. Then I fell asleep, and when I awoke the ship was gone.

I climbed to the top of a lofty tree to see if I could discover anything hopeful, and looking landward I saw something white at a great distance, so I descended from the tree and made my way towards it. As I drew nearer I thought it to be a huge white dome, and when I touched it I found it was so smooth that there was no climbing to the top.

Suddenly the sky became very dark, and I was astonished to find that this was caused by a bird of monstrous size that came flying towards me. I then remembered hearing sailors speak of a miraculous bird called the Roc, and concluded that the great dome must be its egg.

The bird now alighted and sat over the egg, and I noticed that its leg was as thick as the trunk of a tree. I tied myself securely to it with my turban in the hope that next morning the Roc would carry me with her out of this desert island.

My hopes were realised, for as soon as it was daylight the bird flew up so high that I could not see the earth beneath me. Then she descended so quickly that I lost my senses. When I recovered I found myself on the ground, where I speedily untied the knot. Scarcely had I done so when the Roc picked up a large serpent in her bill and flew away with it.

Sinbad the Sailor, from *The Arabian Nights*

1. What did the writer do whilst his friends were gathering flowers and fruits?

2. What did he discover when he awoke from his sleep?
3. How did he get a better view of his surroundings?
4. What did he see in the distance on the landward side?
5. Why was he unable to climb to the top of this object?
6. What caused the sudden darkening of the sky?
7. What did the Roc do on alighting?
8. How did the writer secure himself to the Roc's leg?
9. What did the writer hope the Roc would do?
10. When were his hopes realised?

 B Choose one of the words inside the brackets to complete the sentence correctly.

1. The boys —— Ken because he was so selfish.
   (admired, envied, despised, applauded, respected)
2. His business was so —— that he was able to retire at an early age.
   (ponderous, prosperous, ominous, luminous, virtuous)
3. The child loved the dog because he was so ——.
   (agile, mobile, fragile, docile, futile)
4. This vase is ——; there is not another like it.
   (antique, rare, artistic, oblique, unique)
5. It was —— that the accused had struck a policeman.
   (presumed, alleged, acknowledged, protested, doubted)

C Write the words needed to complete the similes in the sentences below.

1. The warm sunshine of Italy had made Brian as brown as a ——.
2. Scrooge's partner was as dead as a ——.
3. Don and Roy are as thick as —— at present.
4. Having missed lunch Trevor was as hungry as a —— by tea-time.

5. The wrestler looked as strong as a ——.
6. The Mason twins are as alike as two ——.
7. After attention by the trainer the goalie was as right as ——.
8. Hard training had made the champion as fit as a ——.
9. Money invested in National Savings is as safe as ——.
10. A small wedge under one side of the table made it as steady as a ——.

 D Four of the five adjectives in each row are similar in meaning; the other is different. Write the odd words in a column numbered 1 to 10.

1. huge, vast, colossal, intense, immense
2. courageous, brave, valiant, buoyant, gallant
3. healthful, hygienic, sanitary, wholesome, docile
4. weird, grizzly, ghastly, gruesome, grisly
5. cunning, sly, disobedient, crafty, wily
6. laughable, comical, funny, ridiculous, dismal
7. shameless, brazen, ignorant, barefaced, impudent
8. servile, calm, peaceful, serene, placid
9. frank, drunk, open, candid, plain
10. feeble, weak, frail, robust, infirm

 E From the verb **laugh** we form the noun **laughter**. Write the nouns which correspond to the following verbs.

1. perform   6. depart
2. excite   7. defend
3. pursue   8. defy
4. include   9. abolish
5. advise   10. injure

68

Look at these five words:

apple, orange, blossom, pear, plum

All the words except **blossom** are the names of fruits, so **blossom** is out of place. Say which word in each group below is out of place.

1. chair, table, wardrobe, window, sideboard
2. ale, cheese, milk, lemonade, coffee
3. beach, oak, pine, ash, willow
4. cricket, rugby, hockey, baseball, chess
5. grocer, fishmonger, tailor, bankrupt, butcher

 Write a composition of about 15 lines on any one of the following subjects.

1. When I Was Ill In Bed
2. Things Which Please My Mother
3. Gipsies

Comprehension

THE LITTLE DUKE'S ESCAPE

Richard could hardly eat for excitement, while Osmond hastily
made his arrangements, girding on his sword, and giving Richard
a dagger to put in his belt.   He placed the provisions in his wallet,
and then told Richard to lie down on the straw which he had
brought in. "I shall·hide you in it," he said, "and carry you through
the hall, as if I was going to feed my horse."

From the interior of the bundle Richard heard Osmond open
the door; then he felt himself raised from the ground; Osmond was
carrying him downstairs.   The only way to the outer door was
through the hall, and here was the danger.   Richard heard loud
singing and laughter, as if feasting was going on; then someone
said, "Tending your horse, sir?"

"Yes," Osmond made answer, "since we lost our grooms the
poor black would come off badly if I did not attend him myself."

Richard felt himself carried down the steps, across the court; and
then he knew, from the darkness and the changed sound of
Osmond's tread, that they were in the stable.

Osmond laid the living heap of straw across the saddle and
bound it on, then led out the horse, gazing round cautiously as he
did so; but the whole of the people of the castle were feasting, and
there was no one to watch the gates.   Richard heard the hollow
sound of the horse's hoofs as the drawbridge was crossed, and
knew that he was free.

The Little Duke by Charlotte M. Yonge

1. Why was Richard hardly able to eat?

2. How were Richard and Osmond armed?

3. Where were the provisions carried?

4. In what was Richard hidden when he was smuggled out of the castle?

5. What lay between Richard's room and the outer door?

6. How did Richard know that they had reached the stable?

7. What did Osmond do when they reached the stable?

8. Why was there no one watching the gates?

9. How did Richard know that they were crossing the drawbridge?

10. How did Osmond explain the fact that he was feeding his horse himself?

B Complete each sentence below by using one of these words:

| weight | steak | waist | practice | stationery |
| wait | stake | waste | practise | stationary |

1. Paul tied a length of cord round his —— to keep his trousers up.

2. A thick —— was driven into the ground to support the young apple tree.

3. The turkey we had last Christmas was 5 kilograms in ——.

4. Our soccer forwards must —— shooting on the run.

5. We had a long —— at the station, for the train was very late.

6. A —— car is one which is not moving.

7. An old proverb says, "—— not, want not."

8. Our soccer forwards must have more —— at shooting on the run.

9. The hungry driver ate a huge meal of fried —— and onions.

10. Many people use printed —— for their correspondence.

The abbreviations in these sentences are often seen in the sports columns of newspapers. Write the words for which they stand.

1. The Scotland **v.** All Blacks match was refereed by Ivor David.
2. Hutton was out **l.b.w.** to Walker.
3. The sports were run under **A.A.A.** rules.
4. The final of the **F.A.** Cup is played at Wembley Stadium.
5. In the second innings England were 146 for 6 **dec.**

 From the four words in brackets in each sentence select the one which is correctly spelt.

1. Treasure Island is my (favourite, favorite, favorate, favourate) book.
2. We were all (disapointed, disappointed, dissapointed, dissappointed) with the Show.
3. The Education (Commitee, Committe, Comittee, Committee) will meet next Tuesday.
4. The boys and girls are in (separite, separrate, separate, seperate) rooms.
5. The accident (occured, ocurred, occurred, ocured) in the school playground.

Fill the spaces below with words which name the sounds made by the various objects.

1. the —— of an anvil
2. the —— of coins
3. the —— of a whip
4. the —— of steam
5. the —— of a bow
6. the —— of a clock
7. the —— of children's feet
8. the —— of church bells
9. the —— of rusty hinges
10. the —— of a siren

F Below are ten adjectives from which the vowels have been omitted. Look at the definitions carefully, then write the complete words.

1. p * t r * d   = rotten; foul
2. d * r * b l *   = lasting a long time
3. m * r k *   = dark; gloomy
4. g r * t * s   = free of charge
5. f l * x * b l * = easily bent
6. p * l t r *   = trifling; almost worthless
7. s * c * * b l * = fond of company
8. * l * r t   = wide-awake; watchful
9. p * t h * t * c = arousing pity
10. n * t * r * * * s = well-known for something bad

G Write a composition of about 15 lines on any one of the following subjects.

    1. Caught In A Thunderstorm
    2. Homes In Other Lands
    3. When I Go Shopping

TEST 18

 ## Comprehension

A BRAZILIAN FOREST

Birds were there in myriads—and such birds! Their feathers were green and gold and scarlet and yellow and blue. The great toucan, with a beak nearly as big as his body, flew clumsily from stem to stem. The tiny, delicate humming-birds, scarcely larger than bees, fluttered from flower to flower like points of brilliant green. But they were irritable little creatures, and quarrelled with each other and fought like wasps. Green paroquets swooped from tree to tree and chattered joyfully over their morning meal.

Well might Barney and Martin smile with extreme merriment, for monkeys stared at them with expressions of undisguised amazement, then bounded away shrieking and chattering, swinging from branch to branch with incredible speed, and not scrupling to use each other's tails to swing by when occasion offered. Some were big and red and ugly, with blue faces and fiercely grinning teeth; others were delicately formed and sad of countenance, and some were small and pretty, with faces no bigger than a halfpenny. As a general rule, it seemed to Barney, the smaller the monkey the longer the tail.

Martin Rattler by R. M. Ballantyne

1. Which bird had a beak nearly as big as its body?

2. What colour were the humming-birds?

3. In what way did the humming-birds show their irritability?

4. Which birds were happy and talkative?

5. What effect did the monkeys have on Martin and Barney?

6. What effect did Martin and Barney have on the monkeys?

7. What did the monkeys do to each other whilst swinging from branch to branch?
8. What colour were the ugly monkeys?
9. What struck Barney as very strange about the monkeys' tails?
10. What was the size of the face of the smallest monkey?

 Insert an apostrophe (') in each of the following:

1. the monkeys paw
2. mens underwear
3. the ladys waist
4. a mans work
5. the childrens mother

6. the monkeys tails
7. the girls school
8. the childs mother
9. ladies pyjamas
10. the girls face

C Complete each sentence, using the opposite of the word in heavy type.

1. The diamonds in the necklace are **artificial**, but those in the ring are ——.
2. There were several **deep** pools in the river, but some parts of it were quite ——.
3. The Rovers' **attack** was thrustful, but their —— was pitifully weak.
4. Years ago service with the armed forces was **voluntary**; now it is ——.
5. Fruit is **plentiful** in autumn, but very —— in spring.

 Fill in the blanks in each sentence with the words in brackets.

1. John —— scored —— many runs —— Frank ——. (as, has)
2. Will says that —— father —— expecting —— new car next week. (is, his)

3. I —— be glad if you —— reply as soon as possible. (will, shall)

4. —— were several children waiting with —— mothers. (there, their)

5. I can —— that clock ticking from ——. (here, hear)

 The following letter from Robin to Gerald contains several spelling mistakes. Write the correct form of each word which is wrong.

                                              16 Station Road,
                                              Enford,
                                              July, 29th, 1976

Dear Gerald,

      Last Wendesday Farther and Mother went to the adress your parents gave us to look for rooms for the holidays. The landlady was most curteous, but she was suprised to hear that we needed three seperate rooms, and told us that she could not accomodate us. We were very disapointed, but later we found suitable rooms in a large house with a beatiful view of the beach.

      I will tell you more about it when I see you next week.

                                              Best wishes,
                                              Yours sincerly,
                                              Robin

F Complete the following well-known proverbs.

1. A bird in the hand ....

2. A friend in need ....

3. A penny saved ....

4. All's well ....

5. A stitch in time............................

6. Better late ....

76

7. Fine feathers make.........................
8. Where there's a will ....
9. Penny wise ....
10. Still waters ....

 Write a composition of about 15 lines on any one of the following subjects.

                        1. Lumbering
                        2. Sport In Winter
                        3. Ways Of Heating A Room

A

Comprehension

TICKLER

When I ran home from the churchyard the forge was shut up, and Joe was sitting alone in the kitchen. Joe and I being fellow-sufferers, Joe imparted a confidence to me the moment I raised the latch of the door and peeped in at him sitting in the chimney-corner.

"Mrs Joe has been out a dozen times looking for you, Pip. And she's out now, making it a baker's dozen."

"Is she?"

"Yes, Pip," said Joe, "and what's worse, she's got Tickler with her."

At this dismal news I looked in great depression at the fire. Tickler was a wax-ended piece of cane, worn smooth by collision with my tickled frame.

"She sat down," said Joe, "and she got up, and she made a grab at Tickler, and she Ram-paged out."

"Has she been gone long, Joe?" I asked.

"Well," said Joe, "she's been on the Ram-page this last spell about five minutes. She's a-coming! Get behind the door, Pip, and have the towel between you."

I took his advice. My sister, Mrs Joe, throwing the door wide open, and finding an obstruction behind it, immediately discovered the cause, and applied Tickler to its further investigation.

Great Expectations by Charles Dickens

1. Where was Pip returning from?

2. Where was Joe sitting?

3. In what way was Joe related to Pip?

4. Why did Joe warn Pip that Mrs Joe was looking out for him?

5. What was the "dismal news" that Joe gave to Pip?

6. How many times altogether had Mrs Joe been out looking for Pip?

7. What did Mrs Joe take with her?

8. What advice did Joe give to Pip before Mrs Joe returned?

9. Did Pip follow this advice?

10. What did Mrs Joe do when she discovered Pip?

B Insert the correct word in each blank.

1. Mr Brooks —— us how to add fractions. (learnt, taught)

2. We —— Bill at the soccer match. (saw, seen)

3. Where did you put —— pencils? (those, them)

4. —— you at the party last night? (Were, Was)

5. My answer is different —— yours. (from, to)

C When two words are combined a compound word is formed.

Example: black + smith = blacksmith
light + house = lighthouse

Form compound words by writing other words before or after the following:

1. tooth	6. dock
2. water	7. house
3. foot	8. shop
4. door	9. school
5. wind	10. post

D Use a connecting word, **who, but, which, whose,** etc., to join each pair of sentences into one sentence.

Example 1. Dad could not see the cup-tie **because** he could not get a ticket.

1. Dad could not see the cup-tie. He could not get a ticket.

2. We stood outside Buckingham Palace for hours. We failed to see the Queen.

3. At the hotel we were met by a negro porter. He was extremely polite.

4. Uncle Francis has a poodle. It has won over a hundred prizes.

5. Brian is in the school rugby team. Bill is in the school rugby team.

6. We saw a cyclist. He was carrying a rucksack on his back.

7. The boys saw a policeman. To him they reported the burglary.

8. This morning I found a book. I lost it six months ago.

9. I am going to spend a holiday with my uncle. He keeps a farm in Wales.

10. Helen found the watch. Jane had lost it.

E Insert **I** or **me,** as required, in these sentences.

1. You and —— have been appointed prefects.

2. Mr Wilkins has appointed you and —— prefects.

3. Between you and —— Sam is afraid of Bob.

4. I think you and —— had better be moving.

5. Frank left this message for you and ——.

80

F Write the words which you think should be inserted in the spaces in the passage below.

One hot summer ...(1)... a crow that had ...(2)... flying ...(3)... for a ...(4)... time began to ...(5)... thirsty. So she looked about to see if ...(6)... was any place ...(7)... she could find ...(8)... water. There was no stream near, and as there had not been ...(9)... rain for weeks all the little pools were ...(10)... up.

G Write a composition of about 15 lines on any one of the following subjects.

1. The Wild West
2. My Birthday Party
3. A Big Store

Comprehension

TAKEN BY SURPRISE

Many of the men declared that they had seen the heads of the pirates looking over the ramparts, and that they could not have been very far off, so the two parties of seamen, under their respective officers, once more divided to go in search of them. They wandered about in all directions, but the place seemed deserted, and they found nothing. Perhaps this was because they had no torches, and the night was very dark. Already a few streaks of daylight were appearing in the sky when a trampling of feet was heard, and loud shouts in the distance.

Paddy sprang on boldly to meet the foe, and was instantly knocked head over heels by one of his opponents. He felt as if he had been run through with a bayonet, or something of that sort, though he could not make out exactly where he had been wounded.

There was a terrific shouting in the rear of the enemy, and he had no difficulty in recognising the voices of his shipmates. The shouts came nearer and nearer. He picked himself up to see what had become of the enemy, but they were nowhere to be found. Instead of them, a herd of goats, chased by Mr Thorn's party, and frightened by their shouts, were butting away with heroic valour at everybody who came in their way, while daylight revealed the laughing countenances of his friends, who had seen his overthrow and the enemy which caused it.

Paddy did not mind, however. He rubbed himself over, and finding that he had no bones broken, or any puncture in his body, burst into a loud laugh.

The Three Midshipmen by W. H. G. Kingston

1. What were the sailors looking for?
2. Give two reasons why their search was unsuccessful.
3. What happened to Paddy as he went to meet the foe?

4. What did Paddy think had happened to him?
5. Whose shouts did Paddy hear?
6. What did Paddy see when he picked himself up?
7. What were these creatures doing?
8. What did daylight reveal to Paddy?
9. Why did Paddy rub himself over?
10. What did Paddy do when he found that he was all right?

B Write the verbs which are required to complete the following sentences.

1. The police sergeant was —— to the rank of inspector.
2. Arthur —— to the lady for his clumsiness.
3. The accused was —— to six months' imprisonment.
4. The turntable of the gramophone —— too quickly.
5. The sum of £4·50 was —— from Paul's pay as he was absent on Tuesday.

C Column A below contains ten adjectives; column B contains ten nouns. Match each adjective with its appropriate noun. Write the numbers and letters only.

Example: (thrifty housewife) *Answer:* 1 G

Column A	Column B
1. thrifty	A. invention
2. fragrant	B. slope
3. husky	C. music
4. ingenious	D. flower
5. cordial	E. building
6. dilapidated	F. ocean
7. destructive	G. housewife
8. instrumental	H. welcome
9. tempestuous	I. pest
10. precipitous	J. voice

83

D Insert the ten connecting words given below in the correct spaces in the ten sentences which follow.

unless	if	since	or	although
but	as	until	while	because

1. I will wait here —— you return.

2. We enjoyed our trip —— the weather was cold.

3. I will stay here —— you are getting the tickets.

4. Cecil was late for school —— his watch was slow.

5. We shall lose the train —— we hurry.

6. You won't pass your examination —— you don't work.

7. Would you like some cake —— some trifle?

8. I looked everywhere for my pencil —— failed to find it.

9. I have bought a new football —— I saw you last.

10. —— the weather was so wet we stayed indoors.

E In each example write a word which rhymes with the word in heavy type and which corresponds to the meaning given.

1. **wonder:** a mistake

2. **paint:** strange or odd in an interesting way

3. **earn:** to feel a longing or desire

4. **care:** a strong light which affects the eyes

5. **teach:** to make white by exposure to the sun or by using chemicals

6. **dance:** a quick look

7. **early:** big and strong

8. **please:** a light wind

9. **rash:** to strike the teeth together

10. **nod:** to poke with something pointed

84

F Complete the words beginning with **un**—and ending with **—able** in these sentences.

1. The business does not show a profit.
   (The business is un——able.)

2. Dad's car cannot be relied upon.
   (Dad's car is un——able.)

3. The delay cannot be avoided.
   (The delay is un——able.)

4. Our School Journey to Paris is not to be forgotten.
   (Our School Journey to Paris is un——able.)

5. The accused man is in a position which is not to be envied.
   (The accused man is in an un——able position)

G Write a composition of about 15 lines on any one of the following subjects.

1. The Day Of The Week I Enjoy Most
2. How I Would Spend £10
3. Shopping At The Butcher's

Comprehension

THE NEW HOME

In spite of all we had done previously we still found a great deal to do to render our new home really comfortable. The great drawback was the want of light. The cave had only four openings —the door, one window in our kitchen, another in the workshop, and one which lighted the sleeping-rooms. When the entrance door was closed, all at the back, including the stables, were in almost total darkness.

To remedy this I fixed a tall bamboo-cane firmly in the ground (near the centre of the cave), the upper end reaching to the roof. Jack then climbed to the top of it with a pulley and a stake, which he fastened to a cleft in the rock. A long string was passed through the pulley, and to it I fastened a lamp which we had brought from the wreck. My wife filled it with clear oil, and as it had four wicks it furnished a fair amount of light. By means of the rope and pulley we could place it at a convenient height above our heads, or lower it on to the table.

Swiss Family Robinson by J. R. Wyss

1. What was the great drawback in the new home?

2. How many windows were there in the cave?

3. What happened when the entrance door was closed?

4. Where was the tall bamboo-cane fixed?

5. Who climbed to the top of this bamboo-cane?

6. What was the pulley fastened to?

7. What was passed through this pulley?

8. From where had the lamp been obtained?

9. Why did the lamp give a fair amount of light?

10. Why could the lamp be placed at a convenient height above the heads of the dwellers in the cave?

B   Write the missing words in the following sentences.

1. The thief disappeared very quickly.
   (The thief disappeared in the —— of an eye.)
2. The speaker was talking nonsense.
   (The speaker was talking through his ——.)
3. Valerie was born rich.
   (Valerie was born with a —— spoon in her mouth.)
4. The traveller was deliberately murdered.
   (The traveller was murdered in cold ——.)
5. Martin does things without first thinking about them.
   (Martin does things on the —— of the moment.)

C   In each line below one word is wrongly spelt. Find the wrong words, then write them correctly in a column, numbered 1 to 10.

1. boundary	secondary	libary	salary
2. armament	Parlament	testament	ornament
3. abundant	defendant	pendant	independant
4. acceptible	digestible	credible	visible
5. dominate	obstinate	definate	terminate
6. numerous	murderous	thunderous	wonderous
7. gorgious	gracious	precious	delicious
8. poster	imposter	foster	monster
9. disappoint	disallow	disatisfy	disagree
10. shield	shriek	siege	sieze

Rewrite the words in these sentences which require capital letters.

1. lord nelson was killed at the battle of trafalgar.
2. On tuesday the prime minister leaves for america.
3. on christmas day uncle george gave me a pound note.
4. jimmy dale recited a poem entitled the donkey.
5. large crowds gathered outside buckingham palace to see the queen.

 Look at these ten adjectives.

lenient	strenuous
buoyant	emphatic
ravenous	counterfeit
prosperous	indomitable
boisterous	approximate

Write the numbers 1 to 10 in a column, then write opposite each number the word required to complete the sentence.

1. In winter European wolves have been known to become so —— that they enter villages in search of food.
2. An —— answer is one which is nearly, but not quite right.
3. The runner was exhausted by his —— efforts.
4. A —— judge is one who is merciful.
5. The conquest of Everest was made possible by the —— courage of the expedition.
6. The —— sea drove the little ships into port.
7. Charles answered the accusation with an —— denial.
8. By hard work and thrift the grocer had built up a very —— business.
9. A —— substance is one which floats easily, like cork.

10. Thousands of —— coins were found in the cellar of the old mansion.

Write the numbers 1 to 10 in a column, and opposite each write the letter which indicates the title of the book in which the character of that number appears.

Character	Book
1. Mr Squeers	A. Treasure Island
2. Amyas Leigh	B. Nicholas Nickleby
3. Bully Flashman	C. A Tale of Two Cities
4. Miss Betsey Trotwood	D. Martin Rattler
5. David Balfour	E. A Christmas Carol
6. Blind Pew	F. The Jungle Book
7. Tiny Tim	G. Kidnapped
8. Bob Croaker	H. Westward Ho!
9. Sydney Carton	I. Tom Brown's Schooldays
10. Rikki-tikki-tavi	J. David Copperfield

Write a composition of about 15 lines on any one of the following subjects.

1. Red Indians
2. Racing Cars
3. Milk, The Perfect Food

Comprehension

BIG-END VERSUS LITTLE-END

Our histories of six thousand moons make no mention of any other regions than the two great empires of Lilliput and Blefuscu, which two mighty powers have been engaged in a most obstinate war for six-and-thirty moons past.

It began upon the following occasion: it is allowed on all hands that the primitive mode of breaking eggs, before we eat them, was upon the larger end; but his majesty's grandfather, while he was a boy, going to eat an egg, and breaking it according to the ancient practice, happened to cut one of his fingers; whereupon the emperor, his father, published an order commanding all his subjects, upon great penalties, to break the smaller end of their eggs.

The people so highly resented this law that our histories tell us that there have been six rebellions raised on that account; wherein one emperor lost his life and another his crown. These civil commotions were constantly fomented by the monarchs of Blefuscu; and when they were quelled, the exiles always fled for refuge to that empire. It is computed that eleven thousand persons have at several times suffered death rather than submit to break their eggs at the smaller end.

Gulliver's Travels by Dean Swift

1 What two great empires are named in this extract?

2. For how long had they been at war?

3. What was the primitive way of breaking eggs open?

4. Who cut his finger whilst breaking open an egg?

5. What did this boy's father do to prevent such an accident happening again?

6. Why were there six rebellions?
7. By whom were these rebellions started?
8. What happened to two emperors during these rebellions?
9. To what country did the exiles go after the rebellions?
10. Why did the eleven thousand people suffer death?

B There is one punctuation mark missing from each of these sentences; insert it.

1. The police have a warrant for the mans arrest.
2. "Where have you put the rubber Tom?" asked Mary.
3. Have you ever read the story of Sleepy Hollow
4. The elephant crashed its way through the jungle
5. Manfield, the grocer has been taken to hospital.
6. "Look out" yelled Norman. "Here comes the bull!"
7. "You look dead tired, said Sid to his father.
8. Philip cant shoot with his left foot.
9. "Tom," said Mother, "its time for you to go."
10. Miss Harris is twenty four years of age.

C Below you will find the definitions of ten nouns, all of which begin with the letter **t**. Write the words in a column in your exercise book.

1. the small lever which is pulled in firing a gun
2. a ship specially constructed for carrying cargoes of oil
3. a small cap worn on a finger to protect it when pushing a needle in sewing
4. an instrument which makes distant objects appear closer and larger
5. a violent storm with very high winds

6. the arms or feelers of an octopus
7. a person who pays rent for the use of a house, flat, farm, etc.
8. a kind of axe once used as a weapon by Red Indians.
9. either end of a railway, bus route, etc.
10. the carriage which is attached to the rear of a locomotive and is used for carrying coal

 The word **pupil** can mean:

    (a) someone who is being taught
    (b) the tiny, dark circle in the centre of the eye

Write the word which corresponds to each pair of meanings below.

1. (a) a tropical tree
   (b) part of your hand
2. (a) water supply
   (b) part of a watch or clock
3. (a) a place of worship
   (b) part of the side of your head
4. (a) a famous wine
   (b) a haven for ships
5. (a) a fish
   (b) the bottom of your foot

 In each sentence below an adverb can be used in place of the words in heavy type. Make a list of these adverbs, remembering that each ends with —**ly.**

Example: The grocer handled the eggs **with care.**
Answer: carefully

1. The full-back tackled the centre-forward **with vigour.**

2. The work had been done **with skill.**

3. Cyril worked all the sums **with ease.**

4. Grandpa was seated **in comfort** in the armchair.

5. The firemen fought the blaze **like heroes.**

6. The school sports are held **every year.**

7. The boys just wandered about **without any aim.**

8. The tropical sun shone **without pity** on the heads of the weary travellers.

9. James left the room **in a hurry.**

10. The man behaved **like a brute** towards his wife.

 Homonyms are words which are pronounced alike, but which are spelt differently and have different meanings.

Examples: sail, sale
steal, steel

Write the **homonyms** of the twenty nouns which appear below.

1. boy	6. vale	11. mail	16. die
2. fir	7. leak	12. sight	17. cue
3. fowl	8. night	13. bell	18. place
4. rain	9. key	14. feet	19. muscle
5. sole	10. hair	15. break	20. time

Write a composition of about 15 lines on any one of the following subjects.

1. School Meals

2. Wild Birds Of Britain

3. How Rooms Are Ventilated

Comprehension

THE COURT OF JUSTICE

The King and Queen of Hearts were seated on their throne, with a great crowd assembled about them—all sorts of little birds and beasts, as well as the whole pack of cards: the Knave was standing before them, in chains, with a soldier on either side to guard him; and near the King was the White Rabbit, with a trumpet in one hand and a scroll of parchment in the other. In the very middle of the court was a table, with a large dish of tarts upon it: they looked so good that it made Alice quite hungry to look at them. "I wish they'd get the trial done," she thought, "and hand round the refreshments!" But there seemed to be no chance of this so she began looking about her to pass the time away.

Alice had never been in a court of justice before, but she had read about them in books, and she was quite pleased to find that she knew the name of nearly everything there. "That's the judge," she said to herself, "because of his great wig."

The judge, by the way, was the King; and as he wore his crown over the wig he did not look at all comfortable, and it was certainly not becoming.

"And that's the jury-box," thought Alice, "and those twelve creatures," (she was obliged to say "creatures", you see, because some of them were animals and some were birds) "I suppose they are the jurors." She said this last word two or three times over to herself, being rather proud of it: for she thought that few girls of her age knew the meaning of it at all.

Alice's Adventures in Wonderland by Lewis Carroll

1. Where were the King and Queen seated?
2. What was remarkable about the assembly around them?
3. Who was the prisoner?

4. How was the prisoner guarded?
5. Name the two things which the White Rabbit held.
6. What was on the table in the centre of the court?
7. What effect did the sight of these have on Alice?
8. What did Alice do to pass the time away?
9. How did Alice recognise the judge although she had never been in a court of justice before?
10. Why did Alice call the jury "creatures"?

 Ten verbs have been taken out of the following passage and arranged in a different order. Write the numbers 1 to 10 in a column, and opposite each write the verb which will fit correctly into the space with the corresponding number.

These are the ten verbs:

threw	dashed
continued	recovered
scampered	thrown
broke	whirling
followed	reined

Suddenly a herd of wild cattle ...(1)... out of the grove and ...(2)... over the plain, ...(3)... by a man on horseback. ...(4)... the noose of his lasso above his head he ...(5)... it so skilfully that a bull put one of its legs within the coil. Then he ...(6)... up suddenly and the animal was ...(7)... on to its back. At the same moment the lasso ...(8)... and the bull ...(9)... its feet and ...(10)... its wild flight.

C Combine each pair of sentences below into one sentence.

Example: We met a sailor.   He had been shipwrecked.
We met a sailor who had been shipwrecked.

1. Mary laid the table.   She cut bread-and-butter.

2. Dad looked everywhere for his pipe. He could not find it.
3. Harry missed the last bus. He had to walk home.
4. Harry had to walk home. He missed the last bus.
5. We sympathised with Paul. He had damaged his new bicycle.

D Below are ten words from which the vowels have been omitted. Write the complete words in order, 1 to 10, in your exercise book.

1. * n t * r t * * n = to please or amuse
2. d * t * s t = to hate or dislike very much
3. c * l c * l * t * = to find the cost of something by means or arithmetic
4. * n f l * t * = to fill a balloon, football, etc. with air or gas
5. c * n s * m * = to eat, drink, burn, or use up
6. d * s p * r s * = to scatter
7. r * v * * l = to show or display
8. p * n * t r * t * = to go into or through
9. m * t * n * = to rebel against authority
10. g r * v * l = to humble oneself by crawling at a person's feet

E Write in a column the words which are needed to complete these sentences correctly.

1. Our television set is very similar —— yours.
2. This material is different —— the one we had last time.
3. Mother shared the chocolate —— Moira and Sally.
4. Without hesitation the sailor dived —— the sea.
5. Thousands of people died —— the plague in 1665.
6. The headmaster was angry —— Tom.

7. The headmaster was angry —— Tom's behaviour.
8. The farmer shared the apples —— the four boys.
9. I prefer this book —— the one I read last.
10. Several boys failed the examination —— Fred.

F The word **mustn't** is a contraction, or shortened form, of the two words **must not.** Write the contractions of the words in heavy type in these sentences.

1. I **cannot** find my fountain pen.
2. I looked in my satchel but it **was not** there.
3. Children **are not** allowed to smoke.
4. The cuckoo **does not** make a nest for itself.
5. Lupins are pretty flowers but they **do not** last very long.
6. I hope I **shall not** be late for school.
7. Farmer Dale **will not** allow strange dogs inside his farmyard.
8. Cyril pushed and pulled, but **could not** move the heavy crate.
9. Bill and Eddie **were not** in school today.
10. The boys say that they **have not** seen the lost ball.

G Write a composition of about 15 lines on any one of the following subjects.

1. **Wild Flowers**
2. **Eskimos**
3. **Indoor Games I Enjoy**

TEST 24

Comprehension

THE HUNTER

On his head the hunter wore a fur cap of otter-skin, with a flap on each side to cover the ears, the frost being so intense in these climates that, without some such protection, they would inevitably freeze and drop off.

As the nose is constantly in use for breathing it is always left uncovered. Several efforts have been made to construct some sort of nose-bag, but without success, owing to the fact that the breath from the nostrils immediately freezes, and converts the covering into a bag of snow or ice.

Round his neck the hunter wore a thick shawl which entirely enveloped the neck and lower part of his face; thus the entire head was almost covered, the eyes, the nose and the cheek-bones alone being visible. He then threw on a coat made of deerskin, over-lapping very much in front, and confined closely to the figure by means of a scarlet worsted belt instead of buttons, and was ornamented round the foot by a number of cuts, which produced a fringe of little tails. Being lined with thick flannel this garment was rather heavy, but very necessary. A pair of blue cloth leggings were next drawn on over the trousers, as an additional protection to the knees.

The feet, besides being peculiarly susceptible to cold, had further to contend with the chafing of the lines which attach them to the snow-shoes, so that special care in their preparation was necessary. First, a pair of duffle socks were wrapped round the feet, which were next thrust into a pair of made-up socks of the same material, and above these were put another pair. Over all was drawn a pair of moccasins made of stout deerskin.

The Young Fur Traders by R. M. Ballantyne

1. Why was the hunter's cap able to protect his ears from the cold?

2. What would happen to the hunter's ears if they were not protected?

3. Why was the hunter's nose not protected from the cold?

4. What did the hunter wear round his neck?

5. What parts of the hunter's face were visible after he had dressed?

6. How was the hunter's coat kept close to his body?

7. Why was this coat so heavy?

8. What were used as an additional protection for the hunter's knees?

9. Name two things against which the hunter's feet had to be protected.

10. How many coverings did the hunter have on his feet?

B The words in the following sentences are not in their correct order. Write each sentence as it should be.

1. Several workmen were wrapping parcels in overalls.

2. A gold watch was lost by a retired schoolmaster with luminous hands.

3. Wanted: A young man to take care of several dogs of good character.

4. A savage dog chased the tramp with long fangs.

5. The director told the traveller to return to the office by telegram.

A large number of verbs end with —**ate.**

Examples: separate, calculate, liberate

Write the verbs ending with —**ate** which are required to complete these sentences.

1. Next week Sir William will —— his 80th birthday.

2. Classroom windows are opened at playtime in order to —— the room.

3. The engineer showed his assistant how to —— the new machine.

4. Frank was the first to —— George on his success at the examination.

5. The headlights of the car could not —— the dense fog.

6. Thousands of British people —— to Australia every year.

7. When people —— they die for lack of air.

8. A pump is used to —— a football or a tyre.

9. When you —— your shoulder you put it out of joint.

10. Arrows were painted on the walls to —— the way to the show.

 Fill the blanks with **did** or **done,** as required.

1. The picture is broken. I don't know who —— it.

2. Elizabeth —— the work exactly as her mother had shown her.

3. After she had —— it her mother gave her five pence.

4. Derek —— his best to take Roger's wicket.

5. Derek has always —— his best at bowling.

100

Match the idioms in the first column with the meanings in the second column. Write the numbers and the letters only.

Example: 1. H

1. to be a dog in a manger	A. to scorn or despise
2. to turn over a new leaf	B. to manage one's own affairs without help
3. to ride the high horse	C. to live within one's means
4. to turn up one's nose	D. to take a step from which there is no turning back
5. to mind one's p's and q's	E. to be possessed of a crazy idea
6. to paddle one's own canoe	F. to be haughty and overbearing
7. to burn one's boats	G. to be a spoil-sport
8. to have a bee in one's bonnet	H. to refuse to give to others what is useless to oneself
9. to make both ends meet	I. to be careful how one behaves
10. to be a wet blanket	J. to lead a better life

 We speak of a flock of sheep. Write the collective noun for each of the following.

1. a —— of cattle
2. a —— of pups
3. a —— of bees
4. a —— of wolves
5. a —— of fish

6. a —— of whales
7. a —— of birds
8. a —— of singers
9. a —— of footballers
10. a —— of savages

 Write a composition of about 15 lines on any one of the following subjects.

1. The Importance Of Coal
2. The Fifth Of November
3. Politeness

Comprehension

HUMPHREY TO THE RESCUE

Humphrey peered into the pit, and thought that he could make out a human figure lying at the bottom. He called out, asking if there was anyone there, and heard a groan in reply. Horrified at the idea that somebody had fallen into the pit and was perishing for want of help he ran for a long ladder, put it down the pit, and then cautiously descended.

On his arrival at the bottom he found the body of a half-clothed lad lying there, so he carried him up the ladder and laid him on the ground at the side of the pit. Recollecting that the watering-place of the herd of cattle was not far off, Humphrey hurried to it and returned with his hat half-full of water. The lad drank eagerly, and in a few minutes appeared much recovered. Presently he attempted to speak, but Humphrey could not understand what he said as he spoke in a low tone and in a foreign tongue, so Humphrey made signs to the lad that he was going away and would soon be back.

Humphrey ran to the cottage as fast as he could and called for Edward, who, after hearing what had happened, went into the cottage to get some milk and some cake, while Humphrey put the pony into the cart. In a few minutes they were on their way to the pit, and on arriving there found the lad still lying where Humphrey had left him. They soaked the cake in the milk, and gave him some. After a time the rescued lad swallowed it pretty freely, and was so much recovered as to be able to sit up. They then lifted him into the cart and drove gently home to their cottage.

The Children of the New Forest by Capt. Marryat

1. What did Humphrey think he could see at the bottom of the pit?
2. What reply did he get when he called out?

3. Why was Humphrey horrified?
4. How did Humphrey get down into the pit?
5. What did he find on reaching the bottom?
6. How did Humphrey bring water to the rescued lad?
7. Why could Humphrey not understand what the lad was saying?
8. How did Humphrey try to make the lad understand him?
9. What food did Humphrey and Edward give the lad?
10. How did they convey him to their home?

B   The missing words in the phrases below are adjectives formed from the nouns denoting the various types of person.

Example: the care of a mother (motherly care)

1. the conduct of a **hero**   (—— conduct)
2. the appetite of a **glutton**   (a —— appetite)
3. the strength of a **giant**   (—— strength)
4. the behaviour of a **coward**   (—— behaviour)
5. the look of a **villain**   (a —— look)
6. the rule of a **tyrant**   (a —— rule)
7. an assault by a **brute**   (a —— assault)
8. the face of an **angel**   (an —— face)
9. the grin of a **rogue**   (a —— grin)
10. the obedience of a **slave**   (—— obedience)

C   Dogs **bark.** Write the noises made by the creatures named below.

1. horses ——   6. frogs ——
2. sheep ——   7. snakes ——
3. doves ——   8. wolves ——
4. lions ——   9. rooks ——
5. owls ——   10. pigs ——

D Complete the unfinished words in the sentences below by adding —**able** or —**ible** as required.

1. The survivor's story was hardly cred——.
2. Jim made a credit—— attempt to beat the school record for the high jump.
3. Bullies are most detest—— people.
4. Milk is a very digest—— food.
5. Sally's new coat has a detach—— hood.
6. The heavy snowfall made several roads impass——.
7. It was imposs—— for traffic to get through the snow.
8. Gardening can be a very profit—— hobby.
9. A revers—— rug is one which can be used on either side.
10. The number 12 is exactly divis—— by 2, 3, 4 and 6.

E Each sentence below contains two adjectives. Write the numbers 1 to 5 in a column, and opposite each write the two adjectives contained in that sentence.

1. It was a cold, windy day when school reopened.
2. Tom bought a new bicycle with dynamo lighting.
3. We stood admiring the massive, marble columns.
4. A still tongue shows a wise head.
5. The little robins pecked at the juicy apple.

F In each example below select the word which is nearest in meaning to the word in heavy type.

1. Mr Bird consulted Sir James Clark, the **eminent** surgeon.

brilliant	famous
experienced	overworked

2. Bruno is a very **docile** dog.

ferocious	well-trained
alert	obedient

3. The policeman was a **vigilant** officer.

intelligent	watchful
ambitious	muscular

4. The reporter wrote a **vivid** description of his adventures.

realistic	humorous
brief	exaggerated

5. The strikers attempted to **intimidate** the workmen.

persuade	bribe
frighten	assault

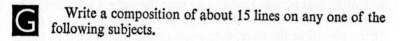 Write a composition of about 15 lines on any one of the following subjects.

1. How I Spend My Pocket Money
2. The Dispersal Of Seeds
3. First Aid In The Home

Comprehension

ROMULUS AND REMUS

To Rhea were born two fair boys; they were twins. Their grand-father, King Amulius, commanded one of his men to take the two children, throw them away, and destroy them. This man, there-fore, put them into a trough, or kind of cradle, and carried them towards the River Tiber, with the intention of throwing them in.

But he found that the river had risen so high, and was running so swiftly, that he was afraid to go near the water's side, and so he laid them on the bank in the trough in which he had carried them. In the meantime the river, ever swelling and overflowing its banks more and more, came underneath the trough, gently lifted it up, carried it into a great plain, and as the waters receded finally left it near a wild fig tree.

To these two children lying there in this manner came a she-wolf and suckled them, and a woodpecker also which helped to nourish them and keep them. These two creatures are now held as sacred to the god Mars.

Faustulus, the chief cowherd to King Amulius, found the two children under the fig tree and took care of them. The two boys, by name Romulus and Remus, were carefully brought up by Faustulus and his wife, being instructed in all honourable things.

The brothers grew up, and in course of time Romulus founded the city of Rome and became its first king.

From *North's Plutarch's Lives*

1. What did King Amulius command one of his men to do with the twins?

2. In what did this man carry the boys away?

3. Where did he take them?

4. What did he intend doing with them?

5. Why did he not carry out his intentions?

6. What happened when the river overflowed its banks?

7. What animal suckled the children?

8. By whom were the twins found?

9. What did this person do with them?

10. What famous city did Romulus found when he grew up?

B The two words missing from each of these sentences are pronounced alike, but spelt differently.

Write the ten pairs of words which will complete the sentences correctly.

Example: Question 1. rode, road

1. The highwayman —— his black mare along the deserted ——.

2. The grass on the race —— was very ——.

3. In the arithmetic test —— children had every —— right.

4. Talking —— should not be —— in libraries.

5. Frank felt a sharp —— as his elbow went through the window ——.

6. I wish you —— chop this —— for me.

7. When cashing a —— you should always —— the amount you receive.

8. Speak up, please; I cannot —— you from ——.

9. In the —— hall of the castle an enormous fire blazed in the ancient ——.

10. On a huge branch of a —— tree crouched a young grizzly——.

107

C The missing words in these sentences are adjectives formed from the names of the countries.

Example: The —— Rugby Team beat the All Blacks. (Wales)
Answer: Welsh

1. The —— flag flew at the masthead. (France)

2. The —— team gave a masterly display of soccer. (Hungary)

3. Every year the —— people send a Christmas tree to London. (Norway)

4. Many men of the —— Air Force remained in Britain after the War. (Poland)

5. We listened attentively to the stories of ancient —— heroes. (Greece)

6. The ship was boarded by —— pirates. (China)

7. A —— bull-fighter was gored by a bull. (Spain)

8. Many —— children still wear the national costume. (Holland)

9. Large quantities of —— timber are now being imported into Britain. (Sweden)

10. A party of —— children competed at the Welsh Eisteddfod. (Denmark)

D Ten words are wrongly spelt in this paragraph. Find them, then write the correct spelling of each.

The peer was almost deserted, but their was a crowd on the key to watch a boat, witch had sprung a leek and torn her sales in the rough whether, come into dock. The crew rode her strait towards the jetty were she was soon safely moored.

E

Look at the participles of these verbs.

> break — broken
> wear — worn
> bite — bitten

Now write the participles of the following verbs.

1. begin	11. ride
2. drink	12. swim
3. give	13. sing
4. write	14. fall
5. take	15. speak
6. draw	16. strike
7. catch	17. strive
8. show	18. tear
9. freeze	19. rise
10. go	20. hurt

F

Match the ten adverbs in the second column with the ten verbs in the first column. Write the numbers and letters only.

Verbs	Adverbs
1. prayed	A. punctually
2. crept	B. gracefully
3. worked	C. ferociously
4. contributed	D. stealthily
5. arrived	E. devoutly
6. spoke	F. profusely
7. danced	G. recklessly
8. bled	H. industriously
9. growled	I. eloquently
10. drove	J. liberally

Write a composition of about 15 lines on any one of these subjects.

1. Spring Cleaning
2. Our Family
3. The Fishing Industry Of Britain

110

A

Comprehension

THE RIVAL SCHOOLS

Mrs Knight's school, to which Katy and Clover and Cecy went, was a low one-storey building, and had a yard behind it in which the girls played at break.   Unfortunately, next door to it was Miss Miller's school, equally large and popular, and with a yard behind it also.   Only a high board fence separated the two playgrounds.

A constant feud raged between the two schools as to the respective merits of the teachers and the instruction.   The Knight girls considered themselves genteel and the Miller girls vulgar, and took no pains to conceal their opinion; while the Miller girls retaliated by being as aggravating as they knew how.   They spent their break mostly in making faces through the knot-holes in the fence, and over the top of it when they could get there, which wasn't an easy thing to do, as the fence was pretty high.

The Knight girls could make faces too, for all their gentility. Their yard had one great advantage over the other: it possessed a wood shed with a climbable roof, which commanded Miss Miller's premises, and upon this the girls used to sit in rows, turning up their noses at the next yard, and irritating the foe by jeering remarks.

"Knights" and "Millerites" the two schools called each other; and the feud raged so high that sometimes it was hardly safe for a Knight to meet a Millerite in the street.

What Katy Did by Susan Coolidge

1. To which school did Katy go?

2. What was the school building like?

3. What lay behind this school?

4. What stood next door to Katy's school?

5. How were the two buildings separated?

6. Why was there a feud between the two schools?

7. How did the Miller girls spend their break?

8. Why was it not easy for them to look over the fence?

9. What advantage did the Knight school yard possess over the Miller school yard?

10. What did the Knight girls do during their break?

 B The pig is a **dirty** animal; the jackal is a **cowardly** creature. In Column A you see the names of ten creatures, and in Column B the adjectives which describe their outstanding characteristics. Match each noun with its correct adjective, writing a number and a letter for each.

Column A	Column B
1. dog	A. mischievous
2. fox	B. proud
3. bee	C. bad-tempered
4. mouse	D. meek
5. peacock	E. obstinate
6. lamb	F. cunning
7. mule	G. wise
8. bear	H. timid
9. monkey	I. faithful
10. owl	J. busy

 C Write the name of each of these characters from literature.

1. The Jew who wanted to cut a pound of flesh off the breast of his debtor.

2. The shipwrecked sailor who lived on a desert island for many years.

3. The little negro girl who said she never was born.

4. The boy who asked for more gruel.

5. The chief of the outlaws of Sherwood Forest.

 One word, a verb, can be used in place of those in heavy type in these sentences. Write the ten verbs in a column.

1. Harold **did as he was told** immediately.

2. Jim did his best to **keep out of the way of** the shopkeeper.

3. The sails of the windmill **turned round and round** slowly.

4. The sea was so rough that the boat **turned upside down.**

5. The tramp was **put into prison** for theft.

6. By the time we reached the top of the hill the climbers had **gone out of sight.**

7. The teacher **said** that Henry's work was **getting better and better** every day.

8. The police called on the burglar to **give himself up.**

9. Fred **made up his mind** to do better next time.

10. The chairman **said he was sorry for** his late arrival.

 In each of the ten phrases below the verb is missing. Fit each of the verbs given into the blank space to which it belongs.

issue	hinder	fulfil	solve	announce
celebrate	declare	forgive	impose	inflict

1. to —— a fine
2. to —— punishment
3. to —— a decision
4. to —— war
5. to —— a statement
6. to —— a promise
7. to —— a wrong
8. to —— a problem
9. to —— progress
10. to —— a victory

F Rewrite the following passage, using the Past Tense of the verbs, which are in heavy type.

Example: The two boys made for the clearing . . .

The two boys **make** for the clearing in the wood, **sit** down on the cool grass, and **begin** to unpack their picnic basket. They **eat** the sandwiches and **drink** the lemonade with relish, then **lie** down and **sleep**. When they **awake** they **rise, go** to the bus stop, and **catch** the bus back to the village.

G Write a composition of about 15 lines on any one of the following subjects.

        1. Lighting A Fire
        2. Cycling
        3. How Animals Defend Themselves

114

Comprehension

THE WILD MAN OF TREASURE ISLAND

My eyes turned in the direction from which the sound had come, and I saw a figure leap with great rapidity behind the trunk of a pine. Whether it was bear or man or monkey I could not tell, but it seemed dark and shaggy, and my terror brought me to a standstill. Then the recollection of my pistol flashed into my mind, and courage glowed again in my heart. Setting my face resolutely towards this man of the island I walked briskly towards him. He was now concealed behind another tree, but he must have been watching me closely, for as soon as I began to move towards him he came to meet me. After some hesitation he came forward, threw himself on his knees, and held out his clasped hands in supplication.

"Who are you?" I asked.

"Ben Gunn," he answered in a hoarse voice. "I'm poor Ben Gunn, I am, and I haven't spoke with a Christian these three years."

I could now see that he was a white man like myself, and that his features were even pleasing. His skin was burnt by the sun; even his lips were black; and his fair eyes looked quite startling in so dark a face.

"Three years!" I cried. "Were you shipwrecked?"

"Nay, mate," said he—"marooned."

I knew that marooning was a horrible punishment common among buccaneers in which the offender is left behind on a desolate island.

"Marooned three years ago," he continued, "and lived on goats since then, and berries and oysters. But, mate, my heart is sore for a Christian diet. You don't happen to have a piece of cheese about you now? No? Well, many's the time I've dreamed of cheese—toasted, mostly—and woke up again, and here I were."

"If ever I can get on board again," said I, "you shall have cheese by the stone."

Treasure Island by Robert Louis Stevenson

1. What did the figure do when the writer looked in that direction?

2. What brought the writer to a standstill?

3. What gave the writer fresh courage?

4. What did the wild man do as the writer moved in his direction?

5. How long had the man been on the island?

6. How had the man come to be on the island for such a long time?

7. What had he lived on all this time?

8. What food did he long for most of all?

9. When would the writer be able to give him what he wanted?

10. Write the sentence which shows that the island had a very hot climate.

 B Write the words in Column A, and opposite each write the word in Column B which matches it.

Example: 1. eagle swooped

Column A	Column B
1. eagle	trotted
2. snake	waddled
3. lamb	hopped
4. mouse	strutted
5. kangaroo	wriggled
6. duck	glided
7. robin	swooped
8. peacock	frisked
9. pony	leaped
10. worm	scampered

116

C Write the proverbs which contain the following pairs of words.

Example: haste, speed
More haste, less speed.

1. come, served
2. vessels, noise
3. miss, mile
4. smoke, fire
5. bitten, shy
6. cooks, broth
7. stone, moss
8. feathers, birds
9. swallow, summer
10. wise, foolish

D Write the verbs which correspond to the following nouns.

Example: success—to succeed

1. assembly   to ——
2. resemblance   to ——
3. satisfaction   to ——
4. invitation   to ——
5. choice   to ——
6. recognition   to ——
7. quotation   to ——
8. admission   to ——
9. pronunciation   to ——
10. exclamation   to ——

From the list of adverbs given choose the one which best describes the action.

anxiously	valiantly	sluggishly	cautiously
politely	distinctly	promptly	reverently
	generously	gratefully	

1. Every speaker should speak ——.

2. In church we should behave ——.

3. We should receive a gift ——.

4. People should give —— to good causes.

5. Over flat land a stream flows ——.

6. For news of her missing son a mother waits ——.

7. A fire brigade should answer a call ——.

8. Soldiers should behave —— in battle.

9. Motorists should take corners very ——.

10. Children should speak —— to their elders.

F Many adjectives end with —ful.

Examples: useful, hopeful, dreadful, awful

For each of the ten adjectives below write an adjective ending with —ful which has a similar meaning.

1. compassionate

2. abundant

3. marvellous

4. detestable

5. dubious

6. injurious

7. extravagant

8. illegal

9. pretty

10. contemptuous

Write a composition of about 15 lines on any one of the following subjects.

1. Road Up—Men At Work
2. A Hospital Nurse
3. A Visit To A Museum

Comprehension

THE CROWNING OF ARTHUR

Merlin the magician felt that the time was come for Arthur to be declared king, so he counselled the Archbishop of Canterbury to call all the barons and the gentlemen-at-arms to come together to London at Christmas time and meet in prayer in the Cathedral of St Paul.

Now when the people came into the church-yard they saw a great sight. There in the space before the church stood a large square stone, like marble, and on the top of it was an anvil of steel a foot high. Through this anvil and into the stone was stuck by the point a beautiful sword, on which were these words written in letters of gold upon the blade:

"Whoso can pull forth this sword out of this stone and anvil is rightly King of all England."

All manner of men tried to pull out the sword, but not one succeeded except Arthur. There, in the presence of them all, he drew out the sword with the utmost ease, and as he did so all the commons cried out, "We want Arthur for our King! We see that it is God's will!"

An angry murmur rose from the barons, and one of them said, "What a boy can do a man can do." So Arthur put the sword back into its place, and every man who wished to try again did so, but not one could withdraw it. Once more Arthur drew forth the sword, and again a great shout arose from the people—"Arthur is King! We will have no King but Arthur!"

Many of the knights and barons were angry at this, but when the Archbishop placed the crown upon the young Prince's head they fell down on their knees at once, and swore to obey him as their lord and sovereign.

Arthur then took the sword in both hands, and offered it on the altar, swearing to be a true king, and to govern with perfect justice all the days of his life.

Le Morte D'Arthur by Sir Thomas Malory

1. Who called the barons and gentlemen-at-arms together?

2. Where did they meet?

3. What was the "great sight" they saw in the churchyard?

4. What inscription did the blade of the sword bear?

5. Who succeeded in withdrawing the sword?

6. Why were the barons angry when the people wanted Arthur for their King?

7. What did Arthur do when he saw their anger?

8. What did the knights and barons do when the Archbishop placed the crown on Arthur's head?

9. What did Arthur do with the sword after he was crowned?

10. What did the new King swear to do?

B Change the following sentences into Indirect Speech.

Example: "I am looking forward to watching television," said June.

June said that she was looking forward to watching television.

1. "Why are you always late for school, William?" asked his teacher.

2. "I have spent all my money," said Margaret.

3. "Let's have a camp fire," suggested Harold.

4. "You have behaved very well, my children," said Mrs Potter.

5. "It is getting dark," observed Martin, "and it is time we went home."

C Insert the following words in the blank spaces after the verb **turned** in these sentences.

out off down round in
over on back up to

1. Very few people turned —— at the meeting.

2. My father turned —— the dealer's offer of £5 for the dresser.

3. The farmer was turned —— of his farm.

4. The sailors, wishing to finish their work early, turned —— with a will.

5. As we were dead tired by 8 o'clock we turned —— for the night.

6. Owing to the drought the water was turned —— for twelve hours every day.

7. Fred just turned —— his heel and walked away.

8. The drunkard turned —— a new leaf after he was married.

9. As I had forgotten my season ticket I turned —— to fetch it.

10. Mrs Grove turned —— to see who was sitting behind her.

D Each sentence below has been divided into five parts, which have been arranged in incorrect order. Write the letters which indicate the correct order.

1. (a) of hundreds of people (b) or buried under avalanches (c) St Bernard dogs (d) who have been lost in blizzards (e) have saved the lives

2. (a) is a world-famous landmark (b) the Rock of Gibraltar (c) above the narrow straits (d) towering fourteen hundred feet (e) where the Mediterranean meets the Atlantic

3. (a) New York was hardly more (b) huddling behind wooden stockades (c) three hundred years ago (d) for protection against Red Indians (e) than a dozen cabins

4. (a) long before printing was invented (b) which is the most interesting part of a monastery (c) copied out by hand (d) often contains beautiful books (e) the library

5. (a) inventors attempted to transmit pictures (b) that J. L. Baird invented the first practical working system (c) but it was not until 1926 (d) for many years (e) over wires or by wireless

E Write the adjectives and verbs which correspond to the nouns below.

Example: haste (n.) hasty (adj.) hasten (v.)

Noun	Adjective	Verb
1. beauty	——	——
2. joy	——	——
3. circle	——	——
4. friend	——	——
5. grief	——	——
6. strength	——	——
7. courage	——	——
8. fright	——	——
9. attention	——	——
10. danger	——	——

F In each line select the verb from the brackets which is most nearly the **opposite** of the verb in heavy type.

1. **praise:** (boast, condemn, reward)
2. **liberate:** (capture, distribute, dismiss)

3. **conclude:** (include, commence, exclude)
4. **reject:** (inject, accept, project)
5. **imperil:** (endanger, neglect, safeguard)
6. **prohibit:** (exhibit, permit, reveal)
7. **diminish:** (complete, begin, increase)
8. **assemble:** (disperse, resemble, gather)
9. **retreat:** (retire, withdraw, advance)
10. **contract:** (attract, subtract, expand)

 Write a composition of about 15 lines on any one of the following subjects.

1. The Police And Their Work
2. A Toy I Made
3. Knitting

Comprehension

THE NEW SCROOGE

Scrooge was early at the office next morning. If only he could be there first, and catch Bob Cratchit coming late! That was the thing he had set his heart upon.

And he did it, yes, he did! The clock struck nine. No Bob. A quarter past. No Bob. He was eighteen and a half minutes behind his time. Scrooge sat with his door wide open, that he might see him come into the tank.

His hat was off before he opened the door, his scarf too. He was on his stool in a jiffy, driving away with his pen as if he were trying to overtake nine o'clock.

"Hallo!" growled Scrooge, in his accustomed voice as near as he could feign it. "What do you mean by coming here at this time of day?"

"I am very sorry, sir," said Bob. "I am behind my time."

"You are?" repeated Scrooge. "Yes, I think you are. Step this way, sir, if you please."

"It's only once a year, sir," pleaded Bob, appearing from the tank. "It shall not be repeated. I was making rather merry yesterday, sir."

"Now, I'll tell you what, my friend," Scrooge said. "I am not going to stand this sort of thing any longer. And therefore," he continued, leaping from his stool and giving Bob such a dig in the waistcoat that he staggered back into the tank again—"and therefore I am about to raise your salary!"

Bob trembled and had the momentary idea of knocking Scrooge down with the ruler and calling for help.

"A Merry Christmas, Bob!" said Scrooge, with an earnestness that could not be mistaken. "I'll raise your salary and endeavour to assist your struggling family."

And Scrooge was better than his word, for he did it all, and infinitely more.

A Christmas Carol by Charles Dickens

1. Why was Scrooge early at the office that morning?
2. Did he succeed in doing what he had planned?
3. How late was Bob Cratchit?
4. What was Bob's excuse for being late?
5. Where was Scrooge sitting when Bob came in?
6. What did Scrooge say he would do to Bob?
7. Why, do you think, did the idea of knocking Scrooge down with the ruler enter Bob's head?
8. Why was this unnecessary?
9. Write the phrase in this extract which shows that Bob was very poor.
10. The word "tank" appears three times in this passage. To what does it refer?

B The missing words in these sentences are verbs which denote movements of parts of the body. Write the ten verbs in a column.

1. Dick —— his fists and faced his opponent.
2. The cornered fugitive —— his teeth in his fury.
3. As he emerged from the cellar into the bright sunshine Ralph —— his eyes.
4. The poor woman —— her hands in despair.
5. Great-grandfather merely —— his shoulders and walked hurriedly away.
6. The half-clad child —— with the cold.
7. The porter —— under the weight of the heavy trunk.
8. Uncle Silas —— his head in agreement.
9. The cat —— her back as the dog approached.
10. Jack sat idly in the armchair —— his thumbs.

Here are the meanings of five well-known proverbs. Write the proverbs correctly.

1. Think well before acting in any matter.
2. Smart clothes make people look very attractive.
3. Never purchase anything which you can't examine beforehand.
4. Learn to do things yourself instead of depending on others.
5. People who move about from one job to another will never become rich.

 You would buy a leg of pork from a butcher. From whom would you buy:

1. tobacco and a pipe
2. a lady's hat
3. materials for writing letters
4. a gold ring
5. a bar of chocolate and some sweets

 Match the words in Column A with those in Column B, writing numbers and letters only.

Example: 8. B (egg-shell — brittle)

Column A	Column B
1. cork	A. absorbent
2. flax	B. brittle
3. leather	C. adhesive
4. health salts	D. inflammable
5. blotting-paper	E. transparent
6. clay	F. buoyant
7. glue	G plastic
8. egg-shell	H. pliable
9. petrol	I. effervescent
10. clear glass	J. fibrous

F Select from the words in the brackets the one which is similar in meaning to the adjective in heavy type.

1. **niggardly:** (foreign, miserly, black)
2. **physical:** (bodily, strong, athletic)
3. **fastidious:** (thoughtful, particular, speedy)
4. **immortal:** (undying, lifeless, deceased)
5. **trivial:** (victorious, trifling, three-cornered)
6. **systematic:** (fortunate, disorderly, methodical)
7. **agile:** (nimble, ancient, breakable)
8. **miscellaneous:** (manufactured, stolen, assorted)
9. **austere:** (severe, gentlemanly, generous)
10. **irksome:** (interesting, tedious, laughable)

G Write a composition of about 15 lines on any one of the following subjects.

1. A Job I Would Like
2. It Was a Dark and Windy Night . . . .
3. A Library I Visit